D0674620

The
Walker's
Anthology

Compiled by
D E B O R A H   M A N L E Y

TRAILBLAZER PUBLICATIONS

The Walker's Anthology
First edition: 2013

Publisher
Trailblazer Publications
The Old Manse, Tower Rd, Hindhead, Surrey, GU26 6SU, UK
www.trailblazer-guides.com

British Library Cataloguing in Publication Data
A catalogue record for this book is available from the British Library

ISBN 978-1-905864-52-2

Editor: Nicky Slade
Layout: Bryn Thomas
Cover image: Come to Britain for Hiking
© Mary Evans Picture Library/Onslow Auctions Limited

DEBORAH MANLEY has lived in India, Canada, Austria and Nigeria.
She worked as an editor of education books and has compiled anthologies
on Malta, the Nile and the Trans-Siberian Railway. She is the co-author of the
biography of the early 19th century traveller and diplomat, Henry Salt, and has
also written articles for the *Guinness Book of Records 1492: The World Five Hundred
Years Ago*. She now lives in Oxford.

Printed on chlorine-free paper by
D'Print (☎ +65-6295 5598), Singapore

CONTENTS

PROCESSIONS AND MARCHES

PILGRIMAGES AND WALKING FOR WORK

WALKING IN WINTER

ON HILLS AND MOUNTAINS

WALKING IN PARKS AND GARDENS

WALKING BY WATER

WALKING IN TOWNS AND CITIES

WALKING AT NIGHT

THE WALKERS

BIBLIOGRAPHY

INDEX

INTRODUCTION

Many centuries ago two people – possibly an adult and a child – walked in soft, muddy ground in the Olduvai Gorge in present day Kenya. And, still walking, the descendants of these two went on to walk right across our world.

Once, of course, walking was the only way to get around. Then people learned to make boats, to use animals and eventually to create motorised transport so as to avoid wasting time and energy on walking. But as leisure time has grown, particularly over the last few centuries, we've rediscovered the pleasure of walking.

Walking can take us to places no car can reach and, of course, one can linger on the way. In towns we can window shop or visit a cathedral or market, or walk in a park. In the countryside there are myriad places that give us serenity, peaceful views and even silence.

All these benefits appear in this collection of walkers' accounts of their journeys through both countryside and towns, by water, and through open country and woodland … in different weathers, at different times of day and of the year.

There are special occasions when we may walk together with others, for example, Trooping the Colour in London, when soldiers and civilians parade through the city streets, thronged along the way by other people who've come to watch and to cheer. Sometimes ordinary people may march for a cause – almost always a political one.

On holiday we may wander through towns and cities or on country roads and paths – sometimes on rising land, on other walks alongside a river or a canal. We need not always have a destination; we may be walking just for pleasure or for exercise.

I have included all these ways of walking in this collection – bringing together the experiences of such famed walkers as Patrick Leigh Fermor on his great walk across Europe, and William Wordsworth and his sister, Dorothy, both in their beloved Lake District and on the continent.

One of the great advantages of travel on foot is that walkers can penetrate almost anywhere: into the forests of West Africa, along the Roman roads of Britain, through the wooded hills of North America, beside water on the tow paths of canals or by a river or along a sea shore.

In bringing together writers for this book I have used a wide variety of sources. I have brought in writing from novels, from children's books and from magazines. I've used travel guides – such as the very detailed, if now somewhat delightfully old fashioned, Baedeker's guides – which very often highlight walks that their readers may wish to make in the countries they visit.

Walking has its own vocabulary: towards the end of a long journey we may 'trudge'. If we walk together in an organised manner or for a special reason we are said to march. If we walk in a leisurely, perhaps unplanned way, we wander.

However we walk and for whatever reason, if we walked through soft mud like that in the Olduvai Gorge long, long ago, we would still leave footprints.

Deborah Manley, Oxford, 2013

SETTING OUT

The start of a walk is an important moment, when things are drawn together, companions chosen, decisions taken and the experience considered …

Setting out, 1879
ROBERT LOUIS STEVENSON

Stevenson had spent time and thought on loading his donkey, Modestine. Now he set out … "and," as he said, "let her go at her own pace, and let me patiently follow."

What that pace was, there is no word mean enough to describe; it was something as much slower than a walk as a walk is slower than a run; it kept me hanging on each foot for an incredible length of time; in five minutes it exhausted the spirit and set up a fever in all the muscles of the leg. And yet I had to keep close at hand and measure my advance exactly upon hers; for if I dropped a few yards into the rear, or went on a few yards ahead, Modestine came instantly to a halt and began to browse. The thought that this was to last from here to Alais nearly broke my heart. Of all the conceivable journeys, this promised to be the most tedious. I tried to tell myself it was a lovely day; I tried to charm my foreboding spirit with tobacco; but I had a vision ever present to me of the long, long roads, up hill and down dale, and a pair of figures ever infinitesimally moving, foot by foot, a yard to the minute, and, like things enchanted in a nightmare, approaching no nearer to the goal.

In the meantime there came up behind us a tall peasant, perhaps forty years of age, of an ironical snuffy countenance, and arrayed in the green tail-coat of the country. He overtook us hand over hand, and stopped to consider our pitiful advance.

"Your donkey," says he, "is very old?"

I told him, I believed not.

Then, he supposed we had come far.

I told him, we had but newly left Monastier.

"Et vous marchez comme ça!" cried he; and, throwing back his head, he laughed long and heartily. I watched him, half prepared to feel offended, until he had satisfied his mirth; and then, "You must have no pity on these animals," said he; and, plucking a switch out of a thicket, he began to lace Modestine about the stern-works, uttering a cry. The rogue pricked up her ears and broke into a good round pace, which she kept up without flagging, and without exhibiting the least symptom of distress, as long as the peasant kept beside us. Her former panting and shaking had been, I regret to say, a piece of comedy.

Travels with a Donkey in the Cévennes (Kegan Paul & Co, London, 1879)

A Walk in the Woods, 1998
BILL BRYSON

Distance changes utterly when you take the world on foot. A mile becomes a long way, two miles literally considerable, ten miles whopping, fifty miles at the very limits of conception. The world, you realize, is enormous in a way that only you and a small community of fellow hikers know. Planetary scale is your little secret.

Life takes on a neat simplicity, too. Time ceases to have any meaning. When it is dark, you go to bed, and when it is light again you get up, and everything in between is just in between. It's quite wonderful, really.

You have no engagements, commitments, obligations, or duties; no special ambitions and only the smallest, least complicated of wants; you exist in a tranquil tedium, serenely beyond the reach of exasperation, "far removed from the seats of strife," as the early explorer and botanist William Bartram put it. All that is required of you is a willingness to trudge.

There is no point in hurrying because you are not actually going anywhere. However far or long you plod, you are always in the same place: in the woods. It's where you were yesterday, where you will be tomorrow. The woods is one boundless singularity. Every bend in the path presents a prospect indistinguishable

Every twenty minutes on the Appalachian Trail, Katz and I walked farther than the average American walks in a week.

from every other, every glimpse into the trees the same tangled mass. For all you know, your route could describe a very large, pointless circle. In a way, it would hardly matter.

At times, you become almost certain that you slabbed this hillside three days ago, crossed this stream yesterday, clambered over this fallen tree at least twice today already. But most of the time you don't think. No point. Instead, you exist in a kind of mobile Zen mode, your brain like a balloon tethered with string, accompanying but not actually part of the body below. Walking for hours and miles becomes as automatic, as unremarkable, as breathing. At the end of the day you don't think, "Hey, I did sixteen miles today," any more than you think, "Hey, I took eight thousand breaths today." It's just what you do."

A Walk in the Woods: Rediscovering America on the Appalachian Trail
(HarperCollins, 1998)

Mole sets out, 1908
KENNETH GRAHAME

It was a cold still afternoon with a hard steely sky overhead, when he slipped out of the warm parlour into the open air. The country lay bare and entirely leafless around him, and he thought that he had never seen so far and so intimately into the insides of things as on that winter day when Nature was deep in her annual slumber and seemed to have kicked the clothes off. Copses, dells, quarries and all hidden places, which had been mysterious mines for exploration in leafy summer, now exposed themselves and their secrets pathetically , and seemed to ask him to overlook their shabby poverty for a while, till they could riot in rich masquerade as before, and trick and entice him with the old deceptions. It was pitiful in a way, and yet cheering – even exhilarating. He was glad that he liked the country undecorated, hard, and stripped of its finery. He had got down to the bare bones of it, and they were fine and strong and simple. He did not want the warm clover and the play of seeding grasses; the screens of quickset, the billowy drapery of beech and elm seemed best away; and with great cheerfulness of spirit he pushed on towards the Wild Wood,

. . . . **Four times I was honked at for having the temerity to proceed through town without the benefit of metal.**
BILL BRYSON *A WALK IN THE WOODS*

which lay before him low and threatening, like a black reef in some still southern sea.

There was nothing to alarm him at first entry. Twigs crackled under his feet, logs tripped him, funguses on stumps resembled caricatures, and startled him for the moment by their likeness to something familiar and far away; but that was all fun and exciting. It led him on, and he penetrated to where the light was less, and trees crouched nearer and nearer, and holes made ugly mouths at him on either side.

The Wind in the Willows (Methuen, London, 1908)

Why are you doing this?, 2010
COLIN THUBRON

"And you? Why are you doing this, travelling alone?"

I cannot answer.

I am doing this on account of the dead.

Sometimes journeys begin long before their first step is taken. Mine, without my knowing, starts not long ago, in a hospital ward, as the last of my family dies. There is nothing strange in this, the state of being alone. The death of parents may bring resigned sadness, even a guilty freedom. Instead I need to leave a sign of their passage. My mother died just now, it seems, not in the way she wished; my father before her; my sister before that, at the age of twenty-one.

Time is unsteady here. Sometimes I am a boy again, trying to grasp the words *Never, never again*. Humans, it is said, cannot comprehend eternity, in time or space. We are better equipped to register the distance spanned by a village drumbeat. The sheerness of *never* is beyond us.

The sherpa's eyes stay mute on me, puzzled. Solitude here is an unsought peril. I joke: "Nobody's fool enough to travel with me!"

It is already evening. Our feet grate over the stones. You cannot walk out your grief, I know, or absolve yourself of your survival, or bring anyone back. You are left with the desire only that things not be as they are. So you choose somewhere meaningful on earth's surface, as if planning a secular pilgrimage. Yet the

Thoughts come clearly while one walks.
THOMAS MANN

meaning is not your own. Then you go on a journey (it's my profession, after all), walking to a place beyond your own history, to the sound of the river flowing the other way. In the end you come to rest at a mountain that is holy to others.

The reason for this is beyond articulation. A journey is not a cure. It brings an illusion, only, of change, and becomes at best a spartan comfort.

To a Mountain in Tibet (Chatto & Windus, London, 2011)

Once upon a time, 1920
FLORA THOMPSON

In the days of her childhood the footpath over the meadow had been a hard, well-defined track, much used by men going to their fieldwork, by children going blackberrying, nutting, or in search of violets or mushrooms, and, on Sunday evenings, by pairs of sweethearts who preferred the seclusion of the fields and copses beyond the more public pathways. The footpath had led to a farmhouse and a couple of cottages, and, to the dwellers in these, it had been not only the way to church and school and market, but also the first stage in every journey. It had led to London, to Queensland and Canada, to the Army depot and the troopship. Wedding and christening parties had footed it merrily, and at least one walking funeral had passed that way.

She herself as a child had trodden it daily, often with her skipping-rope, her white pinafore billowing, her long hair streaming, her feet scarcely touching the ground, or so it seemed to her now. At other times she had carried a basket, on an errand for her mother, to fetch a shillingsworth of eggs, perhaps; eggs twenty a shilling. Not very large eggs, to be sure – they were common barndoor fowls' eggs – but warm from the nest and so full of delicious milky fluid that it pushed from the shell when the egg was tapped for breakfast next morning. Most often of all she had gone that way in her own errands, for a family of cousins had lived in the farmhouse, which, to her, was a second home.

She knew every foot of that meadow by heart. Beneath that further hedgerow violets had grown – white violets and grey

SETTING OUT

blue-veined ones, as well as the more ordinary purple. In spring that dry slope had been yellow with cowslips, short-stemmed cowslips, but honey-sweet of scent. She had once helped to pick a peck of cowslip pips there to make wine, and the flowers and their green rosettes of leaves had felt warm to her hand in the sunshine. The call of the cuckoo had floated over from Brecon Copse, and her mother had told her to wish, because, she had said, if you wish when you hear the first cuckoo of the year your wish will be granted – if reasonable.

Still Glides the Stream (Oxford University Press, 1948)

Starting from Bradford, 1933
J.B. PRIESTLEY

However poor you are in Bradford, you need never be walled in, bricked up, as a round million folk must be in London. Those great bare heights, with a priority of sky above and behind them, are always there, waiting for you. And not very far beyond them, the authentic dale country begins. There is no better country in England. There is everything a man can possibly want in these dales, from trout streams to high wild moorland walks, from deep woods to upland miles of heather and ling. I know no other countryside that offers you such entrancing variety. So if you can use your legs and have a day now and then to yourself, you can never be unhappy long in Bradford. The hills and moors and dales are there for you. Nor do they wait in vain. The Bradford folk have always gone streaming out to the moors. In the old days, when I was a boy there, this enthusiasm for the neighbouring country had bred a race of mighty pedestrians. Everybody went enormous walks. I have known men who thought nothing of tramping between thirty and forty miles every Sunday.

☆ ☆ ☆

You caught the fever when you were quite young, and it never left you. However small and dark your office or warehouse was, somewhere inside your head the high moors were glowing,

All truly great thoughts are conceived while walking.
FRIEDRICH NIETZSCHE

the curlews were crying, and there blew a wind as salt as if it were straight from the middle of the Atlantic. That is why we did not care very much that our city had no charm, for it was simply a place to go and work in, until it was time to set out for Wharfdale or Wensleydale again. We were all, at heart, Wordsworthian to a man. We have to make an effort to appreciate a poet like Shelley, with his rather gassy enthusiasm and his bright Italian colouring; but we have Wordsworth in our very legs.

English Journey (W Heinemann in association with V Gollancz, London, 1934)

Through the forest of Borneo, 1856
ALFRED RUSSEL WALLACE

It is a singular and most interesting sight to watch a Mias (orang-utan) making his way leisurely through the forest. He walks deliberately along some of the larger branches in the semi-erect attitude which the great length of his arms and the shortness of his legs cause him naturally to assume; and the disproportion between these limbs is increased by him walking on his knuckles, and on the palm of the hand, as we should do. He seems always to choose those branches which intermingle with an adjoining tree, on approaching which he stretches out his long arms, and seizing the opposing boughs, grasps them together with both hands, seems to try their strength, and then deliberately swings himself across to the next branch, on which he walks along as before.

He never jumps or springs, or even appears to hurry himself, and yet manages to get along almost as quickly as a person can run through the forest beneath. The long and powerful arms are of the greatest use to the animal, enabling it to climb easily up the loftiest trees, to seize fruits and young leaves from slender boughs which will not bear its weight, and to gather leaves and branches with which to form a nest.

The Malay Archipelago: The Land of the Orang-utan, and the Bird of Paradise
(Harper & Bros, New York, 1869)

I walk slowly, but I never walk backward.
ABRAHAM LINCOLN

SETTING OUT

The old roads of England, 1926
ANTHONY COLLETT

Before the Romans came to fling their great highways over hill and plain, most roads clung to the ridges or the hillsides, and crossed the valley where they were narrowest. All the old roads of England, even the Roman roads, have been dissected during centuries of disuse, and partly abandoned and partly incorporated in fragmentary and piecemeal fashion into later highways and byways. But while the ancient hollow tracks that crept from spring to spring or from one pasture to another are perpetuated in a thousand country lanes, the oldest trails along open hill-tops are mostly left desolate.

The most famous hill-track in England is the route from the dry chalk Hampshire Downs along the North Downs in Surrey to the hills about Canterbury. We call it the Pilgrim's Way, because it was followed in the Middle Ages by pilgrims travelling to the shrine of St Thomas at Canterbury from a large part of the south and west of England, and by others from abroad who landed at Southampton. But the name merely perpetuates its dying purpose. For unknown centuries before Thomas à Becket's time that dry chalk track overlooking the marshy river-bottoms must have been followed by all who moved from east to west, or west to east, through the southern seaboard counties. It is prehistoric, and a more ancient monument than any building.

The road presents both a likeness and a contrast with the second great prehistoric track of southern England – the Ridgeway, or Icknield Way. This runs from the neighbourhood of Stonehenge along the northern crests of the chalk through Berkshire, and then, crossing the Thames, at the ford between Streatley and Goring, pursues its way by a less clearly marked line along the same chalk ridge past Royston and Newmarket into Norfolk. Between three and four thousand years ago that may have been a Pilgrim's Way too, if, as some hold, Stonehenge was a great national temple to which all the tribes of the chalk country flocked annually to a feast of the sun.

The Changing Face of England (Nisbet, London, 1926)

If I could not walk far and fast, I think I should just explode and perish. CHARLES DICKENS

Robinson Crusoe's Island, 1719
DANIEL DEFOE

… The next morning I proceeded upon my discovery; travelling nearly four miles, as I might judge by the length of the valley, keeping still due north, with a ridge of hills on the south and north side of me. At the end of the march I came to an opening, where the country seemed to descend to the west; and a little spring of fresh water, which issued out of the side of the hill by me, ran the other way, that is, due east; and the country appeared fresh, so green, so flourishing, everything being in constant verdure or flourish of spring, that it looked like a planted garden. I descended a little on the side of that delicious vale, surveying it with a secret kind of pleasure, though mixed with my other afflicting thoughts, to think that this was all my own; that I was king and lord of all this country indefensibly, and had a right of possession; and if I could convey it, I might have it in inheritance as completely as any lord of a manor in England. I saw here abundance of cocoa trees, orange, and lemon, and citron trees; but all wild, and very few bearing any fruit, at least not then.

Crusoe gathered fruits and then came the discovery that is his story's great moment.

It happened one day, about noon, going towards my boat, I was exceedingly surprised with the print of a man's naked foot on the shore, which was very plain to be seen on the sand. I stood like one thunderstruck, or as if I had seen an apparition. I listened, I looked round me, but I could hear nothing, nor see anything; I went up to a rising ground to look farther; I could see no other impression but that one. I went to it again to see if there were any more, and to observe if it might not be my fancy; but there was no room for that, for there was exactly the print of a foot – toes, heel, and every part of a foot. How it came hither I knew not, nor could I in the least imagine; but after innumerable fluttering thoughts, like a man perfectly confused and out of myself, I came home to my fortification, not feeling, as we say, the ground I went on, but terrified to the last degree, looking behind

Walking is man's best medicine.
HIPPOCRATES

SETTING OUT

me at every two or three steps, mistaking every bush and tree, and fancying every stump at a distance to be a man. Nor is it possible to describe how many various shapes my affrighted imagination represented things to me in, how many wild ideas were found every moment in my fancy, and what strange, unaccountable whimsies came into my thoughts by the way.

When I came to my 'castle' (for so I think I called it ever after this), I fled into it like one pursued.

The Life and Adventures of Robinson Crusoe (W Taylor, London, 1719)

Walking and its pleasures and ideas, 1850
H. D. THOREAU

I can easily walk ten, fifteen, twenty, any number of miles, commencing at my own door, without going by any house, without crossing a road except where the fox and the mink do: first along by the river, and then the brook, and then the meadow and the woodside. There are square miles in my vicinity which have no inhabitant. From many a hill I can see civilisation and the abodes of man afar. The farmers and their works are scarcely more obvious than woodchucks and their burrows. Man and his affairs, church and state and school, trade and commerce, and manufacture and agriculture, even politics, the most alarming of them all – I am pleased to see how little space they occupy in the landscape. Politics is but a narrow field, and that still narrower highway yonder leads to it. I sometimes direct the traveller thither. If you would go to the political world, follow the great road, follow the market-man, keep his dust in your eyes, and it will lead you straight to it; for it, too, has its place merely, and does not occupy all space. I pass from it as from a bean field in the forest, and it is forgotten. In one half hour I can walk off to some portion of the earth's surface where a man does not stand from one year's end to another, and there, consequently, politics are not, for they are but as the cigar-smoke of a man.

☆ ☆ ☆

I think I cannot preserve my health and spirits unless I spend four

In my afternoon walk I would fain forget all my morning occupations and my obligations to society.
H.D. THOREAU

hours at least, and it is commonly more than that, every day in the open air; sauntering through the woods and over the hills and fields, absolutely free from all worldly engagements. You may safely say, a penny for your thoughts, or a thousand pounds ....

The Selected Essays of Henry David Thoreau (Houghton Mifflin, New York, 1906)

Walking tours, 1876
ROBERT LOUIS STEVENSON

It must not be imagined that a walking tour, as some would have us fancy, is merely a better or a worse way of seeing the country. There are many ways of seeing landscape quite as good; and none more vivid, in spite of canting dilettantes, than from a rail-way train. But landscape on a walking tour is quite accessory. He who is indeed of the brotherhood does not voyage in quest of the picturesque, but of certain jolly humours – of the hope and spirit with which the march begins at morning, and the peace and spir-itual repletion of the evening's rest. He cannot tell whether he puts his knapsack on, or takes it off, with more delight. The excitement of the departure puts him in key for that of the arrival. Whatever he does is not only a reward in itself, but will be further rewarded in the sequel; and so pleasure leads on to pleasure in an endless chain. It is this that so few can understand, they will either be always lounging or always at five miles an hour; they do not play one off against the other, prepare all day for the evening, and all evening for the next day. And, above all, it is here that your over-walker fails of comprehension. ... He will not believe that to walk this unconscionable distance is merely to stupefy and brutalise himself, and come to his inn, at night, with a sort of frost on his five wits, and a starless night of darkness in his spirit.

Not for him the mild luminous evening of the temperate walker! He has nothing left of man but a physical need for a bed-time and a double nightcap; and even his pipe, if he be a smoker, will be savourless and disenchanted. It is the fate of such a one to take twice as much trouble as is needed to obtain happiness, and miss the happiness in the end; he is the man of the proverb, in short, who goes further and fares worse.

I travel not to go anywhere, but to go.
I travel for travel's sake. The great affair is to move.
ROBERT LOUIS STEVENSON

Now, to be properly enjoyed, a walking tour should be gone on alone. If you go in company, or even in pairs, it is no longer a walking tour in anything but name; it is something else and more in the nature of a picnic.

Virginibus Puerisque, and Other Papers (C Kegan Paul, London, 1881)

Up Cameroon Mountain, 20th September, 1895
MARY KINGSLEY

I, with my crew*, keep on up the grand new road the Government is making, which when finished is to go from Ambas Bay to Buea, 3,000 feet upon the mountain's side. This road is quite the most magnificent of roads, as regards breadth and general intention, that I have seen anywhere in West Africa, and it runs through a superbly beautiful country. It is, I should say, as broad as Oxford Street; on either side of it are deep drains to carry off the surface waters, with banks of varied beautiful tropical shrubs and ferns, behind which rise, 100 to 200 feet high, walls of grand forest, the column-like tree-stems either hung with flowering, climbing plants and ferns, or showing soft red and soft grey shafts sixty to seventy feet high without an interrupting branch. Behind this again rise the lovely foothills of Mungo, high up against the sky, coloured the most perfect soft dark blue.

The whole scheme of colour is indescribably rich and full in tone. The very earth is velvety red brown, and the butterflies – which abound – show themselves off in the sunlight, in their canary-coloured, crimson, and peacock-blue liveries, to perfection. After five minutes experience of the road I envy those butterflies. I do not believe there is a more lovely road in this world, and besides, it's a noble and enterprising thing of a Government to go and make it, considering the climate and the country; but to get any genuine pleasure out of it, it is requisite to hover in a bird- or butterfly-like way, for of all the truly awful things to walk on, that road, when I was on it, was the worst.

* The carriers who accompanied her on her journey.

Travels in West Africa (Macmillan & Co, London, 1897)

I don't really think, I just walk.
PARIS HILTON

To most of us the greatest pleasure in walking is when we are in the peaceful countryside and away from roads, traffic and the impact of the modern world.

Escape!, 1899
OSBERT SITWELL

Young children of the well-to-do, like Osbert and Edith Sitwell, often had a governess to teach them.

After these hours were over – and how long the airy vistas of the morning then seemed – our governess would conduct Edith and me for a long walk. In this county, we owned no land, and I learnt here to trespass, instead of being continually trespassed against. Sweet were its joys, the excitement of snatching kingcups with their super-blazed, rich yellow chalices from the marsh, all the time in fear lest a foot should sink into the squelching ground, and still more terrified of the harsh voice of authority; even the bluebells, in reality not nearly so lovely and profuse as those which grow at Renishaw, and the lords-and-ladies, with the Lincoln-green hoods transparent in the deep yellow light of spring, acquired a fresh value if grabbed from under the unseeing eyes of old Mr Eastwood's keepers. No one – we felt sure – and Miss King-Church who we so much loved and revered, finally agreed with us, – no one *could* mind our taking just a few simple wild flowers; and we were, accordingly, much hurt and surprised when one day we were seen and chased out of the woods by an old man shouting, "No trespassers *'ere!*" … After that for a considerable period, I used to feel very uncomfortable when the word 'trespass' occurred in the Morning Service, at church, which I was compelled to attend every Sunday. It was, then, with a peculiar transport of righteous feeling that I loudly reiterated the passage from the Lord's Prayer which runs "As we forgive them that trespass against us ...."

The Scarlet Tree: Being the Second Volume of 'Left Hand, Right Hand!'
(Macmillan, London, 1946)

Glories of the forest, 1863
HENRY WALTER BATES

On leaving the town we walked along a straight suburban road constructed above the level of the surrounding land. It had low swampy ground on each side, built upon, however, and containing several spacious *rocinhas*, which were embowered in magnificent foliage. Leaving the last of these, we arrived at a part where the lofty forest towered up like a wall five or six yards from the edge of the path to the height of, probably, a hundred feet. The tree trunks were only seen partially here and there, nearly the whole frontage from ground to summit being covered with a diversified drapery of creeping plants, all of the most vivid shades of green; scarcely a flower to be seen, except in some places a solitary scarlet passion-flower set in the green mantle like a star. The low ground on the borders between the forest wall and the road was encumbered with a tangled mass of bushy and shrubby vegetation, amongst which prickly mimosas were very numerous, covering the other bushes in the same way as brambles do in England. Other dwarf mimosas trailed along the ground close to the edge of the road, shrinking at the slightest touch of our feet as we passed by. Cassia trees, with their elegant pinnate foliage and conspicuous yellow flowers, formed a great proportion of the lower trees, and arborescent arums grew in groups around the swampy hollows.

After stopping repeatedly to examine and admire, we at length walked onward. The road then ascended slightly, and the soil and vegetation became suddenly altered in character. The shrubs here were grasses, low sedges and other plants, smaller in foliage than those growing in moist grounds. The forest was second growth, low, consisting of trees which had the general aspect of laurels

THROUGH COUNTRYSIDE

After dinner sit awhile, after supper walk a mile.
OLD ENGLISH PROVERB

and other evergreens in our gardens at home: the leaves glossy and dark green...

The sun, now, for we had loitered long on the road, was exceedingly powerful. The day was most brilliant; the sky without a cloud. In fact, it was one of those glorious days which announce the commencement of the dry season. The radiation of heat from the sandy ground was visible by the quivering motion of the air above it. We saw or heard no mammals or birds; a few cattle belonging to an estate down a shady lane were congregated, panting, under a cluster of wide-spreading trees. The very soil was hot to our feet, and we hastened onward to the shade of the forest which we could see not far ahead.

The Naturalist on the River Amazons (John Murray, London, 1863)

Through a Chinese landscape, 1850
ROBERT FORTUNE

The old priest now led me to a different part of the grounds, to see a famous spring. This was in one of the most romantic looking dells or ravines that I had ever beheld. We descended to it by a flight of stone steps, crossed a bridge which spanned the ravine, and found ourselves in front of a small temple. On one side of it the water was gushing down, clear and cool, from the mountain, into a small cistern placed there to receive it; while on the other a cauldron or large kettle was always boiling during the day, in order that tea might readily be made for visitors. Here a number of priests were lounging about, apparently attached to the temple. They received me with great kindness, and begged me to be seated at a table in the porch. (The priests pressed tea upon him.)

After drinking the tea I wandered away along a paved path that led me round the side of the mountain, amidst vegetation which had been planted and reared by the hand of nature alone.

My progress onwards was at last arrested by a steep precipice where the walk ended, and on the top of which a summer-house had been erected. I entered the house and sat down upon one of

Of all exercises walking is the best.
THOMAS JEFFERSON

the benches placed there for visitors. The view which I now obtained was one of the grandest I had seen for many a day. Above me, towering in majestic grandeur, was the celebrated peak of Koo-shan, one thousand feet higher than where I stood. Below, I looked down upon rugged and rocky ravines, in many places barren, and in others clothed with trees and brushwood, but perfectly wild. To afford, as it were, a striking contrast to this scenery, my eye next rested on the beautiful valley of the Min, in which the town of Foo-chow-foo stands. The river was winding through it, and had its surface studded with boats and junks sailing to and fro, and all engaged in active business. Its fields were green, and were watered by numerous canals; while in the background to this beautiful picture were hills nearly as high as Koo-shan, from amongst which the river runs, and where it is lost to the eye.

A *Journey to the Tea Countries of China and India* (John Murray, London, 1852)

Ullswater in Autumn, October, 1769
THOMAS GRAY

A grey autumnal day, the air perfectly calm, and mild, went to see Ullswater, five miles distant ... Walked over a spongy meadow or two, and began to mount the hill through a broad straight green alley among the trees, and with some toil gained the summit. From hence saw the lake opening directly at my feet, majestic in its calmness, clear and smooth as a blue mirror, with winding shores and low points of land covered with green enclosures, white farm houses looking out among the trees, and cattle feeding. The water is almost everywhere bordered with cultivated lands, gently sloping upwards from a mile to a quarter of a mile in breadth, till they reach the foot of the mountains which rise very rude and awful in their broken tops on either hand. Directly in front, at better than three miles distance, Place-fell, one of the bravest amongst them, pushes it bold broad breast into the midst of the lake, and forces it to alter its course, forming first a large bay to the left, and then bending to the right.

I descended Dunmallet again by a side avenue, that was only not perpendicular, and came to Barton bridge, over the Eamont;

... one study found that in regular walkers the hippocampus, an area of the brain essential for memory, actually expanded. Regular walkers have brains that in MRI scans look,

then walking through a path in the wood round the bottom of the hill, came forth where the Eamont issues out of the lake, and continued my way along its western shore, close to the water, and generally on a level with it. Saw a cormorant flying over it and fishing.

Journal of his Tour in the Lake District (1775)

Near home, 1820
JOHN CLARE

And then I walk and swing my stick for joy
And catch at little pictures passing bye
A gate whose posts are two old dotterel trees
A close with molehills sprinkled o'er its leas
A little footbrig with its crossing rail
A wood gap stopt with ivy wreathing pale
A crooked stile each path crossed spinney owns
A brooklet forded by its stepping stones

The Moorhen's Nest (1820)

THROUGH COUNTRYSIDE

In the Rocky Mountains, 1891
BLACKWOOD'S MAGAZINE

These forests of spruce were of a billiard-table green, and in the morning sun they shone with a deliciously tempered hue, relieved and made more beautiful still by the white glistening of the powdery seams above, which divided each lovely mountain-crest from its neighbour. And, brightly emerald green in hue, the Bow River sped in and out through their fair forests below and the roar of the waterfall alone disturbed the silence in the air. At Banff all the land enclosed by the various mountains, twenty six miles long by about ten in width, which is at present all forest, has been set apart by the Canadian Government as a national park.

If, however, one wishes to take a tour in this Rocky Mountain park, it is as well to take a rifle instead of the walking cane of civilisation; for although the frequent Stony Indians whom you come across will not interfere with you, the park is full of bears,

on average, two years younger than the brains of those who are sedentary.
DR MICHAEL MOSLEY & MIMI SPENCER, *THE FAST DIET*

wolves, wolverines and other wild animals. Just before our arrival a police captain slew an enormous black bear at that part of the park abutting on the splendid Cascade Mountain which little hill, by the way, is nine thousand eight hundred feet high, and quite inaccessible from the park itself.

Blackwood's Magazine (1891)

Stormy weather near Llandovery, 1862
GEORGE BORROW

I started at about ten o'clock; the morning was lowering, and there were occasional showers of rain and hail. I passed by Rees Pritchard's church, holding my hat in my hand as I did so, not out of respect for the building, but for memory of the sainted man who of old from its pulpit called sinners to repentance, and whose remains slumber in the churchyard unless washed away by some frantic burst of the neighbouring Towey (River). Crossing a bridge over the Bran just before it enters the greater stream, I proceeded along a road running nearly south and having a range of fine hills on the east. Presently violent gusts of wind came on, which tore the sear leaves by thousands from the trees, of which there were plenty by the roadsides. After a little time, however, this elemental hurly-burly passed away, a rainbow made its appearance, and the day became comparatively fine. Turning to the south-east under a hill covered with oaks, I left the vale of the Towey behind me, and soon caught a glimpse of some very lofty hills which I supposed to be the Black Mountains. It was a mere glimpse, for scarcely had I descried then when mist settled down and totally obscured them from my view.

In about an hour I reached Llangadog, a large village. The name signifies the church of Gadog. Gadog was a British saint of the fifth century, who after labouring amongst his own countrymen for their spiritual good for many years, crossed the sea to Brittany, where he died. Scarcely had I entered Llangadog when a great shower of rain came down. *(He retreated into the warmth of an ancient looking hostelry.)*

Wild Wales: Its People, Language and Scenery (John Murray, London, 1862)

Walking is the best possible exercise. Habituate yourself to walk very fast. THOMAS JEFFERSON

Daffodils, 1807
WILLIAM WORDSWORTH

I wandered lonely as a cloud
That floats on high o'er vales and hills,
When all at once I saw a crowd,
A host, of golden daffodils;
Beside the lake, beneath the trees,
Fluttering and dancing in the breeze.

Continuous as the stars that shine
And twinkle in the milky way,
They stretched in never-ending line
Along the margin of a bay;
Ten thousand saw I at a glance,
Tossing their heads in sprightly dance.

The waves beside them danced; but they
Out-did the sparkling waves in glee;
A poet could not but be gay,
In such a jocund company;
I gazed – and gazed – but little thought
What wealth the show to me had brought;

For often, when on my couch I lie
In vacant or in pensive mood,
They flash upon that inward eye
Which is the bliss of solitude;
And then my heart with pleasure fills,
And dances with the daffodils.

Poems in Two Volumes: Moods of my Mind (1807)

THROUGH COUNTRYSIDE

At Athos, 1794
J.B.S. MORRITT

(Mount) Athos itself, before us, is a still more magnificent object;
its sides, which are covered with wood, terminate in a high pointed crag of an amazing height, which catches the lights of the sun,

I have two doctors, my left leg and my right.
G.M. TREVELYAN

and reflects it in the softest and most brilliant colouring, both in the morning and evening. I have no hesitation in saying that, accustomed as I have been to beautiful scenery, this surpasses any I had ever seen, for the details of it were everywhere as lovely as the *ensemble*. At every step clear springs, rising out of the beds of verdure, dash across the road; at every step you pass trees covered with ivy, every one of which would make a picture; several villages, monasteries, and other decent houses, surrounded each by tufts of trees, or rising out of banks of wood, are seen in the most picturesque points of view; the sea below forms a thousand bays, over which the trees hang on the waters edge; the mountain itself, more uneven than I ever saw, gives you a fresh view at every turn. By this means the scene unites every beauty of the wildest and grandest sort to those of the finest and most fertile countries. The retired scenes of rock and wood are as perfect as the effect of the grand prospects of the country and the islands, and the forest is at the same time full of the finest trees, now in their greatest beauty, and a thick bed of shrubs and flowers. The grass, which had just sprung from the late rains, had the verdure of spring, and the weather was as warm as it is with us in the beginning of September.

The Letters of John B.S. Morritt of Rokeby (Cambridge University Press, 1914)

Spring beauty all around, 1930
WINIFRED FORTESCUE

Never shall I forget that glorious first of May. John led me next morning through the woods which back the house, on and up amid the green gloom of wonderful trees, until suddenly we came out into the sunlight and stood above a sea of primroses, acres of little pale yellow stars washing in yellow waves downhill to a bluebell wood far below.

"The Easter Close," John said simply, and it seemed to me that no more fitting name could have been chosen for that perfect place….

"You are crying, darling?" …

That spring was one of the loveliest that I had ever seen: every

Just watch me walking in all the squares.
A.A. MILNE, *WHEN WE WERE VERY YOUNG* (1924)

flowering shrub was loaded with blossom; the thorn-trees were snow-white; the golden wild azaleas flamed to a height of fourteen feet and scented the air with heady fragrance; the woods and copses were carpeted with bluebells; the meadows yellow with cowslips and primroses; foxglove spears guarded the hedges; golden marsh marigolds and yellow iris fringed the streams.

Perfume from Provence (William Blackwood & Sons, Edinburgh, 1935)

A Walk-about in Australia, 1925
PHILIPPA BRIDGES

The Fincke Creek was scorchingly hot when we watered the camels, and I was glad to leave the glare of the white sand and get on to the Hugh River, where there are lovely gum trees, and as the afternoon waned, we reached the Depot Sand-Hills, camping about four miles south of the Rocky Hill. The sand was as red as brick dust, and the camels floundered about in it. Topsy alighted and caught a sand-devil, a little animal that looked like a large toad, but walked like a lizard, and was clothed in a patchwork of small squares, each with a soft but prickly spine. It carried its little 'swag' on its back, and thrust out its head from a sockety neck like that of a tortoise. It seemed to have no weapon of defence but to make faces. After I had had a good look at it, Topsy put it down again, and it walked into hiding between two inadequate stalks. Later we saw others sitting at the mouths of their tunnels, waiting for us to go by. They all seemed ridiculously tame.

The gum-tree likes a hard bed for its roots, so none grow in the sandhills. The beautiful casuarina, locally called the 'oak', holds sway. It is at its best in the 'soft' country, and I suppose from its long, depending needles with many joints, that it is a beautiful amplification of the ugly little weed called marestail. There are, I believe, twenty varieties of casuarinas, including she-oak, bull-oak, and beefwood.

Throughout my whole trip I had no more lovely camp than that in Depot Sandhills. The wind was cold enough to make me glad of a tent, and the natives built a big fire.

A Walk-about in Australia (Hodder & Stoughton, London, 1925)

The best remedy for a short temper is a long walk.
JOSEPH JOUBERT

Walking in the Desert, 1848
Harriet Martineau

Harriet Martineau found camel riding through the sandy desert from Cairo to the Sinai Peninsula so uncomfortable and utterly exhausting that, when she could, she walked …

THROUGH COUNTRYSIDE

A woman who can walk far and easily, and bear the thirst which is the chief drawback on walking in the desert, may set out for Mount Sinai without fear. I was so far from being injured by my desert travelling, that I improved in health from week to week, after having been unwell in Egypt. There is nothing to fear for a traveller who can walk: but a woman who has no alternative, and must ride her camel all the way, should consider well before she undertakes the journey. – As for all palankeens, panniers, chairs and boxes, – they are wholly insufferable, adding to the evil of the camel-pace, which cannot be got rid of, pains and penalties of their own.

Walking in the Arabian desert is made more easy than in any portion of the desert I saw up the Nile, by the tracks, which are very conspicuous and rarely intermit. During our whole journey from Cairo to Mount Sinai, I saw only three or four places where I should have had any doubt of the road, if I had been alone. The tracks are simply discolourations of the dark pebbly ground or rocky platforms in some places, and a hardening of the sand in others. Sometimes scores of these tracks can be parallel, winding away before and behind, and dying out of sight on either hand, so as greatly to moderate the sense of retreat and solitude in the desert.

I have mentioned, in the camel riding, the only drawback I remember on the pleasure of desert travelling. It is a large item in the account; but my impression of all the rest is now as of one long delight.

Eastern Life (Edward Moxon, London, 1848)

After a day's walk everything has twice its usual value. G.M. Trevelyan

Oliver walks to London, 1838
CHARLES DICKENS

London!—that great place!—nobody—not even Mr. Bumble—could ever find him there! He had often heard the old men in the workhouse, too, say that no lad of spirit need want in London; and that there were ways of living in that vast city, which those who had been bred up in country parts had no idea of. It was the very place for a homeless boy, who must die in the streets unless some one helped him. As these things passed through his thoughts, he jumped upon his feet, and again walked forward.

He had diminished the distance between himself and London by full four miles more, before he recollected how much he must undergo ere he could hope to reach his place of destination. As this consideration forced itself upon him, he slackened his pace a little, and meditated upon his means of getting there. He had a crust of bread, a coarse shirt, and two pairs of stockings, in his bundle. He had a penny too—a gift of Sowerberry's after some funeral in which he had acquitted himself more than ordinarily well—in his pocket. "A clean shirt," thought Oliver, "is a very comfortable thing; and so are two pairs of darned stockings; and so is a penny; but they are small helps to a sixty-five miles' walk in winter time." But Oliver's thoughts, like those of most other people, although they were extremely ready and active to point out his difficulties, were wholly at a loss to suggest any feasible mode of surmounting them; so, after a good deal of thinking to no particular purpose, he changed his little bundle over to the other shoulder, and trudged on.

Oliver walked twenty miles that day; and all that time tasted nothing but the crust of dry bread, and a few draughts of water, which he begged at the cottage-doors by the road-side. When the night came, he turned into a meadow; and, creeping close under a hay-rick, determined to lie there, till morning. He felt frightened at first, for the wind moaned dismally over the empty fields:

THROUGH COUNTRYSIDE

It is not easy to walk alone in the country without musing upon something. CHARLES DICKENS

and he was cold and hungry, and more alone than he had ever felt before. Being very tired with his walk, however, he soon fell asleep and forgot his troubles.

He felt cold and stiff, when he got up next morning, and so hungry that he was obliged to exchange the penny for a small loaf, in the very first village through which he passed. He had walked no more than twelve miles, when night closed in again. His feet were sore, and his legs so weak that they trembled beneath him. Another night passed in the bleak damp air, made him worse; when he set forward on his journey next morning he could hardly crawl along.

In fact, if it had not been for a good-hearted turnpike-man, and a benevolent old lady, Oliver's troubles would have been shortened by the very same process which had put an end to his mother's; in other words, he would most assuredly have fallen dead upon the king's highway. But the turnpike-man gave him a meal of bread and cheese; and the old lady, who had a ship-wrecked grandson wandering barefoot in some distant part of the earth, took pity upon the poor orphan, and gave him what little she could afford—and more—with such kind and gentle words, and such tears of sympathy and compassion, that they sank deeper into Oliver's soul, than all the sufferings he had ever undergone.

Early on the seventh morning after he had left his native place, Oliver limped slowly into the little town of Barnet. The window-shutters were closed; the street was empty; not a soul had awakened to the business of the day. The sun was rising in all its splendid beauty; but the light only served to show the boy his own lonesomeness and desolation, as he sat, with bleeding feet and covered with dust, upon a door-step.

Oliver Twist (Richard Bentley, London, 1838)

A hopeful errand, 1891
THOMAS HARDY

While working at a starve-acre farm Tess hears news of her estranged husband, Angel Clare, and decides she must go and visit his parents at Emminster Vicarage, fifteen miles away. She leaves early on a Sunday morning.

It was a year ago, all but a day, that Clare had married Tess, and only a few days less than a year that he had been absent from her. Still, to start on a brisk walk, and on such an errand as hers, on a dry clear wintry morning, through the rarefied air of these chalky hogs'-backs, was not depressing; and there is no doubt that her dream at starting was to win the heart of her mother-in-law, tell her whole history to that lady, enlist her on her side, and so gain back the truant.

In time she reached the edge of the vast escarpment below which stretched the loamy Vale of Blackmoor, now lying misty and still in the dawn. Instead of the colourless air of the uplands, the atmosphere down there was a deep blue. Instead of the great enclosures of a hundred acres in which she was now accustomed to toil, there were little fields below her of less than half-a-dozen acres, so numerous that they looked from this height like the meshes of a net. Here the landscape was whitey-brown; down there, as in Froom Valley, it was always green. Yet it was in that vale that her sorrow had taken shape, and she did not love it as formerly. Beauty to her, as to all who have felt, lay not in the thing, but in what the thing symbolized.

Keeping the Vale on her right, she steered steadily westward; passing above the Hintocks, crossing at right-angles the high-road from Sherton-Abbas to Casterbridge, and skirting Dogbury Hill and High-Stoy, with the dell between them called "The Devil's Kitchen". Still following the elevated way she reached Cross-in-Hand, where the stone pillar stands desolate and silent, to mark the site of a miracle, or murder, or both. Three miles further she cut across the straight and deserted Roman road called Long-Ash Lane; leaving which as soon as she reached it she

THROUGH COUNTRYSIDE

dipped down a hill by a transverse lane into the small town or village of Evershead, being now about halfway over the distance. She made a halt here, and breakfasted a second time, heartily enough – not at the Sow-and-Acorn, for she avoided inns, but at a cottage by the church.

The second half of her journey was through a more gentle country, by way of Benvill Lane. But as the mileage lessened between her and the spot of her pilgrimage, so did Tess's confidence decrease, and her enterprise loom out more formidably. She saw her purpose in such staring lines, and the landscape so faintly, that she was sometimes in danger of losing her way. However, about noon she paused by a gate on the edge of the basin in which Emminster and its Vicarage lay... She took off the thick boots in which she had walked thus far, put on her pretty thin ones of patent leather, and, stuffing the former into the hedge by the gatepost where she might readily find them again, descended the hill; the freshness of colour she had derived from the keen air thinning away in spite of her as she drew near the parsonage.

Tess of the d'Urbervilles: A Pure Woman (Macmillan, London, 1891)

The flowers of Norfolk, 1939
LILIAS RIDER HAGGARD

In 1939, people withdrew from cities and waited to see whether War would come and what, if it came, it would bring. The countryside gave comfort with its changing beauty ...

In the long meadow at the top of the Vineyard Hills a little patch of the shrubby Rest Harrow has broken out into pinky purple blossom. Our ancestors used the root peeled and infused it for jaundice and dropsy. Ever since I was a child that patch had been there, but the plant is not to be found anywhere else on the farm. The habitat of certain plants has always puzzled me. Why does it grow there and nowhere else, and being there why does it never spread? The same can be said of a clump of giant teazles which appear every autumn in the hedge nearby. On the old cart track

A vigorous five-mile walk will do more good for an unhappy but otherwise healthy adult than all the medicine and psychology in the world. PAUL DUDLEY WHITE

down to the headland overlooking the valley you will find the pale mauve scabious and the blue corn chicory – they have always been there. In a certain garden in the Close at Norwich that 'plant of Greate Virtue', comfrey, is a plague, resisting all efforts to get rid of it. Transplanted to my wild garden and considered in every way I have the greatest difficulty in keeping it. Why does the curious little Pellitory-of-the-Wall always grow on old churches, and where there is a history of monastic occupation (some walls at Blakeney are covered with it). They are all part of the endless problems anyone taking a single step in the country with his eyes open is confronted with.

Norfolk Notebook (Faber & Faber, London, 1946)

Round Dubrovka, 1937
J.B. PRIESTLEY

In Russia there were 'free-days' every sixth day of the month.

I spent many of these free-days exploring the country round Dubrovka, going for long tramps through the snow, at first with Harry or with German friends; later, when I got to know them and their language, with Russian friends from the works.

The forests, fir, pine, and occasional silver birch, stretched for miles on every side, and in the winter, with their branches bowed down with snow and with the frosty, blue sky overhead, these forests bore eloquent testimony to the origins of the Russian fairy stories and folk-lore. The forests, though apparently limitless, were carefully marked out with regular series of boundary posts. For the safety of travellers, pieces of red cloth had been tied on to the higher branches of trees at intervals along the paths in case these were obliterated in heavy snow-storms.

☆ ☆ ☆

In the summer the walking became easier as the snow-drifts melted away, but it was often too hot to think of walking and I was content to spend my free time either at the river or sun-bathing in the hammock on my balcony.

In my long walks in the country in spring I was surprised to

THROUGH COUNTRYSIDE

**Any man that walks the mead
In bud, or blade, or bloom, may find
A meaning suited to his mind.** LORD TENNYSON

note how little the flowers, birds, and animals differed from those in England. I saw foxes and hares, squirrels and hedgehogs, and all the common birds like rooks, crows and sparrows. On one journey I saw a magpie* but was relieved to reflect that superstition has been abolished in the Soviet Union.

* When one sees a magpie it can bring good or bad luck according to an old saying: "One for sorrow, two for joy, three for a girl and four for a boy…"

Rain Upon Godshill, A Further Chapter of Autobiography (Heinemann, London, 1939)

To a secret and lovely place, 1938
MARJORIE KINNAN RAWLINGS

The novel The Yearling *draws us vividly into the life of Jody, his pet fawn and the southern American woodlands.*

He slowed down to make the road last longer. He had passed the big pines and left them behind. Where he walked now, the scrub had closed in, walling in the road with dense sand pines, each one so thin it seemed to the boy it might make kindling by itself. The road went up an incline. At the top he stopped. The April sky was framed by the tawny sand and the pines. It was as blue as his home-spun shirt, dyed with Grandma Hutto's indigo. Small clouds were stationary, like bolls of cotton. As he watched, the sunlight left the sky a moment and the clouds were grey.

"There'll come a little old drizzly rain before the night-fall," he thought.

The down grade tempted him to a lope. He reached the thick bedded sand of the Silver Glen road. The tar-flower was in bloom, and fetter-bush and sparkleberry. He slowed to a walk, so that he might pass the changing vegetation tree by tree, bush by bush, each one unique and familiar. He reached the magnolia tree where he had carved the wild-cat's face. The growth was a sign that there was water nearby. It seemed a strange thing to him, when earth was earth and rain was rain, that scrawny pines should grow in the scrub, while by every branch and lake and river there grew magnolias. Dogs were the same everywhere, and oxen and mules and horses. But trees were different in different places.

Walking and talking are two very great pleasures, but it is a mistake to combine them. Our own noise blots out the sounds and silences of the outdoor world; and talking

"Reckon it's because they can't move none," he decided. They took what food was in the soil under them.

The east bank of the road shelved suddenly. It dropped below him twenty feet to a spring. The bank was dense with magnolia and loblolly bay, sweet gum and grey-barked ash. He went down to the spring in the cool darkness of their shadows. A sharp pleasure came over him. This was a secret and lovely place.

The Yearling (Charles Scribner's Sons, New York, 1938)

Into pre-history, 1850
BAYARD TAYLOR

In California Taylor walked through the forests of the 'Big Trees'.

How cool, and silent, and balmy was the stupendous forest, in the early morn! Through the open spaces we could see a few rosy bars of vapour far aloft, tinted by the coming sun, while the crimson and golden sprays of the undergrowth shone around us, like "morning upbreaking through the earth!" the dark red shafts soared aloft rather like the great circular watch-towers of the Middle Ages, than any result of vegetable growth.

We wandered from tree to tree, overwhelmed with their bulk, for each one seemed more huge than the last. Our eyes now comprehended their proportions. Even the driver (who had brought them there) at first said, "They're not so – *condemned* big, after all!" now walked along silently, occasionally pacing around a trunk, or putting his hand upon it, as if only such tangible proof could satisfy him.

☆ ☆ ☆

During our walk, we watched the golden radiance of the sun, as, first smiting the peaks of the scattered giants, it slowly descended, blazing over the a hundred feet of their massive foliage, before the tops of the enormous pines were touched. This illumination first gave us a true comprehension of their altitude. While sketching afterwards from the veranda, the laws of perspective furnished a new revelation. The hostess and my wife, standing

leads almost inevitably to smoking, and then farewell to nature as far as one of our senses is concerned.

C.S. LEWIS

together at the base of the tree, became the veriest dwarfs. Beyond them what appeared to be a child's toy-cart – in reality the wagon of an emigrant family which had arrived the evening before!

Eldorado, or, Adventures in the Path of Empire (George P Putnam, New York, 1850)

Green-tinted in the Black Forest, 1880
MARK TWAIN

From Baden-Baden we made the customary trip into the Black Forest. We were on foot most of the time. One cannot describe those noble woods, nor the feeling with which they inspire him. A feature of it is a buoyant, boyish gladness; and a third and very conspicuous feature of it is one's sense of the remoteness of the work-day world and his entire emancipation from it and its affairs.

These woods stretch unbroken over a vast region; and everywhere they are such dense woods, and so still, and so piney and fragrant. The stems of the trees are trim and straight, and in many places all the ground is hidden for miles under a thick cushion of moss of a vivid green colour, with not a decayed or ragged spot on its surface, and not a fallen leaf or twig to mar its immediate tidiness. A rich cathedral gloom pervades the pillared aisles; so the stray flecks of sunlight that strike a trunk here and a bough yonder are strongly accented, and when they strike the moss they fairly seem to burn. But the weirdest effect, and the most enchanting, is that produced by the diffused light of the low afternoon sun; no single ray is able to pierce its way in, then, but the diffused light take colour from moss and foliage, and pervades the place like a faint green-tinted mist, the theatrical fire of fairyland. The suggestion of mystery and supernatural which haunts the forest is intensified by the unearthly glow.

A Tramp Abroad (American Publishing Co, 1880)

A journey is best measured in friends, rather than miles. TIM CAHILL

In the West African forest, 1893
MARY KINGSLEY

We gradually get into a more beautiful type of country, and forest. The high trees are the usual high forest series with a preponderance of acacias. It is a forest of varied forms, but flowerless now in the dry season. There are quantities of ferns; hart's-tongues and the sort that grows on the oil-palms, and the elkshorn growing out of its great brown shields on the trees above, and bracken, and pretty trailing lycopodium climbing over things, but mostly over the cardamoms which abound in the under-bush, and here and there great banks of the most lovely ferns I have ever seen save the tree-fern, an ambitious climber, called, I believe, by the botanists *Nephrodium circutarium*, and walls of that strange climbing grass, and all sorts of other lovely things by thousands in all directions.

Butterflies and dragon-flies were scarce here compared to Okijon, but of other flies there were more than plenty.

The roadway is exceedingly good; certainly in the grass country you are rather liable to what Captain Evershield graphically describes as "stub your toe" against lava-like rock, for the grass has overgrown the road, leaving only a single-file path open. In the forest you come across isolated masses of stratified rock, sometimes eight and ten feet high, most prettily overgrown with moss and fern.

Travels in West Africa (Macmillan & Co, London, 1897)

To the farm, 1887
FLORA THOMPSON

When Charity was old enough to be trusted out alone, she was often sent to the farm.

"Now be sure not to get run over," her mother would say, snapping the elastic of her hat under her chin, and she would promise to be careful, though it would have been difficult for a

If your dog is fat, you're not getting enough exercise.
ANON

much more venturesome child than her to have got itself run over on a road where the most dashing equipage was the Manor House wagonette with, between its shafts, the old grey mare, which at other times pulled the lawn-mower. The doctor's gig, an occasional farm wagon, the baker's van, or the coalman's cart were the only other wheeled vehicles she was likely to meet. She might see a horseman or a horsewoman, a tinker with his barrow, or a herd of cows ambling peacefully homeward towards milking time, but seldom anything more dangerous. Once, indeed, on a grey misty September morning, she had suddenly been confronted by a large flock of geese being driven by road to market. She had not stopped to say "Bo!" to them, but had crept between the lower rails of a field gate, for she knew that geese had a nasty way of stretching out their necks and hissing at small girls. When they had passed and she had ventured out of the field, she found the wet road patterned all over with webbed foot-prints, and that pleased her.

Still Glides the Stream (Oxford University Press, 1948)

The flowers of the pine forest in the Jura, 1849
JOHN RUSKIN

Patiently, eddy by eddy, the clear green streams wind along their well-known beds; and under the dark quietness of the undisturbed pines, there spring up, year by year, such company of joyful flowers as I know not the like of among all the blessings of the earth. It was spring-time too; and all were coming forth in clusters crowded for very love; there was room enough for all, but they crushed their leaves into all manner of strange shapes only to be nearer to each other. There was the wood anemone, star after star, closing every now and then into nebulae; and there was the oxalis, troop by troop, like virginal processions of the Mois de Marie, the dark vertical clefts in the limestone choked up with them as with heavy snow, and touched with ivy on the edges – ivy as light and lovely as the vine; and, ever and anon, a blue gush of violets and cowslip bells in sunny places; and in the more open ground, the vetch, and comfrey, and mezereon, and the

Away, away, from men and towns,
To the wild wood and the downs,
To the silent wilderness,

small sapphire buds of the Polygala Alpina, and the wild strawberry, just a blossom or two, all showered amidst the golden softness of deep, warm amber-coloured moss.

I came out presently on the edge of the ravine; the solemn murmur of the waters rose suddenly from beneath, mixed with the singing of the thrushes among the pine boughs; and, on the opposite side of the valley, walled all along as it was by grey cliffs of limestone, there was a hawk sailing slowly off their brow, touching them nearly with his wings, and with the shadows of the pines flickering upon his plumage from above; but with the fall of a hundred fathoms under his breast, and the curling pools of the green river gliding and glittering dizzily beneath him, their foam globes moving with him as he flew …

The Seven Lamps of Architecture: The Lamp of Memory (Smith, Elder & Co, London, 1849)

The heaths and scents of Suffolk, 1950
WILLIAM ADDISON

For one man who revels in the marshes, a hundred revel in the heaths, and these are continuous along at least three-fifths of the Suffolk coast. There are patches between Lowestoft and Gorleston, and between the Deben and the Blyth there is one vast heath, broken only by modern plantations and a few small efforts of cultivation. It is a remarkable tract of wild country to find in the highly cultivated counties of England. As I think of the Suffolk heath I am a little surprised to find that it is the scent of it that comes first to mind. The sense of smell I have always thought the most intimate of senses. We all know the joy of seeing a loved village again, the joy of hearing the old, familiar sounds and the joy of touching the loved one's hand, but most moving of all is the peculiar scent of each particular place or person. The scent of the heath is peculiar to itself and at the same time variable. In spring the shoots of bracken are young and sharp-scented; in autumn a warm breath rises from the dry, purple heather and the sun-baked earth. The heath is one kind of place in rain and another in sun. But if the scent comes first to mind and touches the heart most closely, the scenes and sounds are no less clear and

(side text, vertical) THROUGH COUNTRYSIDE

**Where the soul need not repress
Its music.**
PERCY BYSSHE SHELLEY

are, perhaps, more lasting. There is the skylark with his 'silver chain of sound', the plaintive notes of the willow warbler and the jingle of the corn bunting. But these sensations are meaningless until you have experienced them. Perhaps they only amount to saying that the Suffolk coast has a strange, indefinable atmosphere, wild and restless and at times foreboding; at other times strong and exhilarating, with a voice that laughs defiance at the sea that threatens it when the wind whistles through the marram grass that mantles the bentlings or sand-dunes; at other times intimate and soothing as a lullaby.

Suffolk (Robert Hale, London, 1950)

In Cameroun, 1894
MARY KINGSLEY

We leave the road about fifty yards above the hut, turning into the unbroken forest on the right-hand side, and following a narrow, slippery, muddy, root-beset bush-path that was a comfort after the road. Presently we come to a lovely mountain torrent flying down over red-brown rocks in white foam; exquisitely lovely, and only a shade damper than the rest of things. Seeing this I solemnly folded up my umbrella and give it to Kefalla. My relations, nay, even Mrs Roy, who is blind to a large percentage of my imperfections, say the most scathing things about my behaviour with regard to water. But really my conduct is founded on sound principles. I know from a series of carefully conducted experiments, carried out on the Devonshire Lynn, that I cannot go across a river on slippery stepping-stones; therefore, knowing that attempts to keep my feet out of water only end in my placing the rest of my anatomy violently in, I take charge of Fate and wade.

This particular stream, too, requires careful wading, the rock over which it flows being arranged in picturesque, but perilous confusion; however all goes well, and getting to the other side I decide to 'chuck it', as Captain Davis would say, as to keeping dry, for the rain comes down heavier than ever.

Now we are evidently dealing with a foot-hillside, but the rain is too thick for one to see two yards in any direction, and we

Walking is good for solving problems — it's like the feet are little psychiatrists. TERRI GUILLEMETS

seem to be in a ghost-land forest, for the great palms and red-woods rise up in the mists before us, and face out in the mist behind, as we pass on. The rocks which edge and strew the path at our feet are covered with exquisite ferns and mosses – all the most delicate shades of green imaginable, and here and there of absolute gold colour, looking as if some ray of sunshine had lingered too long playing on the earth, and had got shut off from heaven by the mist, and so lay nestling among the rocks until it might rejoin the sun.

The path now becomes an absolute torrent, with mud-thickened water, which cascades round one's ankles in a sportive way, and round one's knees in the hollows of the path.

Five minutes after abandoning the umbrella I am wet through, but it is not uncomfortable at this temperature, something like that of a cucumber frame with the lights on, if you can clear your mind of all prejudice, as Dr Johnson says, and forget the risk of fever which saturation entails.

On we go, the path underneath the water seems a pretty equal mixture of rock and mud, but they are not evenly distributed. Plantations full of weeds show up on either side of us, and we are evidently now on the top of a foot-hill. I suspect a fine view of the sea could be obtained from here, if you have an atmosphere that is less than 99 per cent of water. As it is, a white sheet – or more properly speaking, considering its soft, stuffy woolliness, a white blanket – it stretched across the landscape to the south-west, where the sea would show.

Travels in West Africa (Macmillan & Co, London, 1897)

On Ulinish, 1785
JAMES BOSWELL

Wednesday, September 22 – In the morning I walked out, and saw a ship, the Margaret of Clyde, pass by, with a number of emigrants on board. It was a melancholy sight. After breakfast we went to see what was called a subterranean house, about a mile off. It was upon the side of a rising ground. It was discovered by a fox having taken up his abode in it, and in chasing him, they dug it out.

The human spirit needs places where nature has not been rearranged by the hand of man. ANON

It was very narrow and low, and seemed about forty feet in length. Near it, we found the foundations of several small huts, built of stone. Mr M'Queen who is always for making everything as ancient as possible, boasted that it was the dwelling of some of the first inhabitants of the island, and observed, what a curiosity it was to find here a specimen of the houses of the aborigines, which he believed could be found nowhere else; and it was plain that they lived without fire.

Dr Johnson remarked that they who had made this were not in the rudest state, for that it was more difficult to make it than to build a house …

The Journal of a Tour to the Hebrides (J. Debrett, London, 1785)

A windy day in Easedale, 1801
DOROTHY WORDSWORTH

Tuesday, 24th … It was very windy, and we heard the wind everywhere about us as we went along the lane, but the walls sheltered us. John Green's house looked pretty under Silver How. As we were going along we were stopped at once, at the distance of perhaps 50 yards from our favourite birch tree. It was yielding to the gusty wind with all its tender twigs, the sun shone upon it, and it glanced in the wind like a flying sunshiny shower. It was a tree in shape, with stem and branches, but it was like a Spirit of water. The sun went in, and it resumed its purplish appearance, the twigs still yielding to the wind, but not so visibly to us. The other birch trees that were near it looked bright and cheerful, but it was a creature by its own self among them …

We went through the wood – it became fair. There was a rainbow which spanned the lake from the island-house to the foot of Bainriggs. The village looked populous and beautiful. Catkins are coming out; palm trees budding; the alder, with its plum-coloured buds. We came home over the stepping stones. The lake was foamy with white waves. I saw a solitary butter-flower in the wood … Reached home at dinner time.

Journals of Dorothy Wordsworth (Macmillan & Co, London, 1897)

There is nothing like walking to get the feel of a country. A fine landscape is like a piece of music; it must be taken at

Walking with the Brontës, 1985
CHRISTOPHER SOMERVILLE

In Britain there are many places where one can walk – so to speak – in the footsteps of a person from the past. In his Twelve Literary Walks, *the author takes his reader up lanes, across bridges and out into country apparently little changed since the earlier walker experienced it …Here, he takes the reader where the Brontës would have walked a century and more ago. Haworth is a place where the shadow of the Brontë family is strong across the land … though the modern world has introduced changes into the route …*

The walk starts in the cobbled lane outside the Parsonage and passes the next extension behind the main building by a sign marked 'Haworth Moor'. A path paved with flagstones hollowed by countless pilgrims' feet leads across the field – the way is often extremely muddy, and a pair of Aunt Branwell's pattens would not come amiss here. At the bottom corner of the field you join West Lane by a narrow stone stile, and fork left fifty yards up the road. The route follows the tarmac road beneath a massive slab of rock engraved Penistone Hill Country Park. On the hillside to the left is Haworth Cemetery; on the right, the ridge-top village of Stanbury, where dry stone field walls marking the boundaries of medieval strip fields curve in parallel lines above the flat waters of Lower Laithe Reservoir, built in 1925.

The road from Stanbury to Oxenhope is crossed at a green wooden sign, Public footpath to Brontë Waterfalls, beyond which a cattle grid gives access to a tarred lane which winds past deserted farmhouses into open moorland, following a favourite walk of the Brontë sisters. The sodden peat-hags on the left of the lane, speckled with bright green sphagnum moss, disgorge water in a hundred streamlets, filling the air with the constant sound of trickling water which competes with a walker's attention in the solitude of the moors with the bleating of the tough black-faced sheep, the trilling of larks, and the bubbling cry of curlews. The ruined farmhouses with their solid mullioned windows and barns built of a piece with the main living quarters bear silent

THROUGH COUNTRYSIDE

the right tempo. Even a bicycle goes too fast.
PAUL SCOTT MOWRER, *THE HOUSE OF EUROPE*

witness to the harshness of conditions up here; the majority of the high moorland farmers have been forced down to lower levels by rain, wind, poor communications and poorer ground ...

Twelve Literary Walks (WH Allen, London, 1985)

In the forests with the Assiniboine, 1864
Viscount Milton and Dr Cheadle

Travelling across Canada in the mid-19th century, Milton and Cheadle had now reached western Canada in the winter. They were invited to go hunting with the local people.

As soon as it became light we prepared for the hunt. The woman and the boy were to accompany us in order to search for the beaver which the Assiniboine had killed the night before, Mr O'B, to his infinite dismay, being left alone in charge of the camp. He remonstrated strongly ...

We proceeded under the guidance of the Assiniboine to the scene of his adventure the previous evening. There we found every detail of his narrative confirmed – the rotten tree trunks torn asunder, the huge foot-prints of the bears in the soft soil or long grass, worn into a beaten track where they had so repeatedly charged up to him, his own track as he took the circuitous route to his second position behind the logs; and leading away from the place, the marks of the three bears going off at speed. It appeared, however, that they had not left the neighbourhood until that morning, for we found very fresh tracks crossing the stream, and on the opposite bank, a wet line marked by the drippings from the shaggy coats of the animals after emerging from the water.

We followed on, the Assiniboine leading, at a great pace, yet with wonderful stillness, through the thick underwood, finding from time to time fresher and still fresher signs – a rotten log newly torn, a bees' nest just dug up, and footmarks in which the grass seemed still rising after the removal of the pressure. We were in a high state of excitement, stealthily advancing, with guns cocked and bated breath, expecting every moment to see

I want to walk through life instead of being dragged through it. **Alanis Morissette**

their terrible forms close to us, when we came upon a hard, grass-less stretch of ground, where the men were unable to follow the tracks, and, after a long search, were, much to our chagrin, compelled to give up the pursuit.

The North-West Passage by Land (Cassell, London, 1865)

Walking with history, 1910
E.L. BUTCHER

Every evening we tied up against the bank (of the Nile) and walked on shore, or sat to watch the sunset colour all the west with crimson fire. We bought our supplies as we went of fresh meat, poultry, eggs and vegetables, and once or twice in the voyage we waited contentedly near some village while the crew made and baked a fresh supply of bread. Sometimes a halt was called to examine one of those forgotten cemeteries which honeycomb the desert for miles and miles in so many places, the resting-place of all the countless unnamed dead who could not afford the costly chapels and stone sarcophagi of nobles, priests and kings. Even so far away from 'civilisation' almost all those at all near the Nile have been ransacked and despoiled by the native antiquity dealers. The openings yawn dangerously at your feet except where years of sand have partly hidden the work of sacrilegious hands. A few shreds of grave-clothing, the broken boards of the coffin, are all that remain to bear witness to the piety of the ancient Egyptian and the greed of his latter-day descendants; though, indeed, tomb-robbing seems to have been a fairly common offence even in the old days.

.... We paused for a day at a ruined, but still inhabited town, and in the course of a morning's walk could find inscribed stones belonging to its walls or temples, with 3000 years between the earliest and the latest date, while stone Christian coffins which held the dead of Clement's time now serve as troughs for water.

Things Seen in Egypt (Seeley, London, 1910)

THROUGH COUNTRYSIDE

Asthall and 'Black Stockings', 1906
F. G. BRABANT

Some roads – before the days of motor cars – acquired a mysterious character....

Asthall is a village on the Windrush, one mile north of the Witney and Burford road. About four miles from Witney the road makes a descent to Worsham Bottom, a spot full of supernatural terrors in the old coaching days, for it was thought that on dark and stormy nights 'Black Stockings', a little evil-faced figure clad in dark velvet and hose, suddenly sprang out and grabbed at the horses' reins.

A little farther on the road ascends to Asthall Barrow, an ancient landmark, now banked up with stone and crowned with a dark fir-clump. The Roman road, Akeman Street, ran close by, passing through the village, which is a mile off, and reached by taking the turning to the right. It is one of the most attractive of Oxford villages, the handsome church and fine restored Elizabethan manor-house standing close together, on a well-wooded slope stretching down to the Windrush.

Oxfordshire (Methuen, London, 1906)

The Duddon Valley, 1910
KARL BAEDEKER

We may be accustomed to reading modern copies of the Baedeker Guides to Europe, but may not be familiar with his detailed guide to our own country, published in 1910.

The easiest way to visit this valley, immortalized by Wordsworth in his Sonnets to the Duddon, is to take the train to Broughton-in-Furness or drive by coach to Seathwaite or walk thence along the river. It may be reached also by the path over the Walne Scar to the south of the Old Man, with the ascent of which it may be combined.

The Duddon rises near the Wrynose Pass, 14 miles above Broughton, where its sandy estuary begins, and forms the bound-

It is impossible to walk rapidly and be unhappy.
MOTHER TERESA OF CALCUTTA

ary between Cumberland and Lancashire. At Ulpha (Travellers' Rest Inn, good), 5½ miles above Broughton, the route to Dalegarth Force, Eskdale and Wast Water diverges to the left. About 2½ miles farther on is Seathwaite Church (rebuilt) of which "Wonderful Walker" was rector for 67 years (1735-1802), governing his parish with "an entirely healthy and absolutely autocratic rule", leading the way in all manual labour as well as instructing his people in spiritual matters, bringing up and educating eight children, and leaving £2000 – all on an annual stipend of less than £50. He is buried in the churchyard. About half a mile beyond the church the road over the Walna Scar Pass diverges to the right (to Coniston, 5 miles). From this point, too, we may ascend along the Seathwaite Beck to Seathwaite Tarn, and thence to the top of the Old Man.

It is, however, better to follow the Duddon to a point nearly opposite the head of Seathwaite Tarn, and then make for the tarn (¼ mile) straight across country. From the head of the Duddon valley, the Wrynose Pass (1270 feet) leads to the east, past the 'Three shire stone', where Lancashire, Cumberland and Westmorland meet, into Little Langdale, and the Hardknott Pass (1290 feet) leads to the West, past Hardknott Castle, a fairly preserved Roman camp, to Boot in Eskdale. Eskdale may also be reached more directly from the Duddon by a path skirting the south west side of Harter Fell (2140 feet).

Baedeker's *Great Britain* (Karl Baedeker, Leipzig, 1910)

From the Nile in Sudan, 1910
E.S. STEVENS

We went ashore; the men to shoot. A village of tukls looks very much like a collection of hay-ricks, but a close inspection proved them to be clean, although cocks and hens ran in and out as they do in Irish cottages, and small kids, whose mammas were wandering about with the herds outside the village, were given the freedom of the little homesteads. A zariba or protection of thorns often formed a kind of yard about a tukl. The women, swathed in their dark blue robes, came out to gaze and smile at us.

From walking: something; from sitting: nothing.
BULGARIAN PROVERB

One asked where we were going. When we replied, "Fok baid ketir," (Yonder very far), she seemed satisfied. For everyone understands 'Fok' here to mean southwards. Mangy dogs, naked children, and semi-naked girls completed the population of the village. The men were out with the herds.

....Outside the village a sun-baked track led into the surrounding bush. The grey soil of the trodden path was cracked into wide fissures from the heat. Dry, unkempt grass, thorny brake, cassia trees red of stem and protected with spikes, their powdery balls still honey-sweet if one plucked and smelt them, and other trees blighted and sparse – in fact, a barren mockery of a forest – stretched to right and left of this footway. It is as if Nature had exhausted the colours on her palette, and had painted this part of the world in browns and greys and ochres.

Half a mile out, we came upon high-shouldered, meek-looking oxen, tender-eyed as Leah, driven by a herdsman. He was black and unclothed to the loins, and wore a crownless sailor hat after the manner of a halo. After the sound of their scuttering hoofs had died away again, there was silence except for the sound of many wings when flocks of pigeons or wood-doves fluttered up in twenties and thirties, and away.

Then we returned to the village, over which vultures, strong-winged and patient, hovered, watchful for offal. The guns returned too, with guinea fowl, a franklin partridge, small quail, and a blue roller with long tail-feathers. They had seen monkeys and the spoor of a hippo.

My Sudan Year (Mills & Boon, London, 1912)

To the Back Pasture, 1898
RUDYARD KIPLING

You must go down by the brook that feeds the clicking, bubbling water-ram; up through the sugar-bush, where the young maple undergrowth closes round you like a shallow sea; next follow the faint line of an old country road running past two green hollows fringed with wild rose that mark the cellars of two ruined houses; then by Lost Orchard, where nobody ever comes except in

We wander for distraction, but we travel for fulfillment.
HILAIRE BELLOC

THROUGH COUNTRYSIDE

cider-time; then across another brook, and so into the Back Pasture. Half of it is pine and hemlock and spruce, with sumach and little juniper-bushes, and the other half is grey rock and boulder and moss, with green streaks of brake and swamp; but the horses like it well enough – our own and others that are turned down there to feed at fifty cents a week. Most people walk to the Back Pasture, and find it very rough work; but one can get there in a buggy, if the horse knows what is expected of him.

From a short story entitled *The Walking Delegate* in *The Day's Work*
(Macmillan & Co, London, 1898)

Visiting Mr Darcy, 1813
JANE AUSTEN

Breakfast was scarcely over when a servant from Netherfield brought the following note for Elizabeth:

"MY DEAREST LIZZY,—I find myself very unwell this morning, which, I suppose, is to be imputed to my getting wet through yesterday. My kind friends will not hear of my returning till I am better. They insist also on my seeing Mr. Jones—therefore do not be alarmed if you should hear of his having been to me—and, excepting a sore throat and headache, there is not much the matter with me.—Yours, etc."

"Well, my dear," said Mr. Bennet, when Elizabeth had read the note aloud, "if your daughter should have a dangerous fit of illness—if she should die, it would be a comfort to know that it was all in pursuit of Mr. Bingley, and under your orders."

"Oh! I am not afraid of her dying. People do not die of little trifling colds. She will be taken good care of. As long as she stays there, it is all very well. I would go and see her if I could have the carriage."

Elizabeth, feeling really anxious, was determined to go to her, though the carriage was not to be had; and as she was no horsewoman, walking was her only alternative. She declared her resolution.

"How can you be so silly," cried her mother, "as to think of such a thing, in all this dirt! You will not be fit to be seen when

The distance is nothing when one has a motive.
ELIZABETH BENNETT IN *PRIDE AND PREJUDICE*

you get there."

"I shall be very fit to see Jane—which is all I want."

"Is this a hint to me, Lizzy," said her father, "to send for the horses?"

"No, indeed, I do not wish to avoid the walk. The distance is nothing when one has a motive; only three miles. I shall be back by dinner."

"I admire the activity of your benevolence," observed Mary, "but every impulse of feeling should be guided by reason; and, in my opinion, exertion should always be in proportion to what is required."

"We will go as far as Meryton with you," said Catherine and Lydia. Elizabeth accepted their company, and the three young ladies set off together.

"If we make haste," said Lydia, as they walked along, "perhaps we may see something of Captain Carter before he goes."

In Meryton they parted; the two youngest repaired to the lodgings of one of the officers' wives, and Elizabeth continued her walk alone, crossing field after field at a quick pace, jumping over stiles and springing over puddles with impatient activity, and finding herself at last within view of the house, with weary ankles, dirty stockings, and a face glowing with the warmth of exercise.

She was shown into the breakfast-parlour, where all but Jane were assembled, and where her appearance created a great deal of surprise. That she should have walked three miles so early in the day, in such dirty weather, and by herself, was almost incredible to Mrs. Hurst and Miss Bingley; and Elizabeth was convinced that they held her in contempt for it. She was received, however, very politely by them; and in their brother's manners there was something better than politeness; there was good humour and kindness. Mr. Darcy said very little, and Mr. Hurst nothing at all. The former was divided between admiration of the brilliancy which exercise had given to her complexion, and doubt as to the occasion's justifying her coming so far alone. The latter was thinking only of his breakfast.

Pride and Prejudice (T. Egerton, London, 1813)

I like long walks, especially when they are taken by people who annoy me. Noël Coward

PROCESSIONS AND MARCHES

3

There are formal occasions for walking – or processing – when a group of people, or perhaps just a few people, walk together on organised occasions to celebrate some present or past occasion.

Marching past the Sultan, c. 1650
EVLIYA ÇELEBI

A thousand and one guilds marched past the Sultan's kiosk by the Great Porte.

All these guilds pass on wagons or on foot, with the instruments of their handicraft, and are busy with the great noise of their work. The carpenters prepare wooden houses, the builders raise walls, the wood-cutters pass with loads of trees, the sawyers pass sawing them, the masons whiten their shops, the chalk-makers crunch chalk and whiten their faces, playing a thousand tricks.

The toy-makers of Eyüp exhibit on wagons a thousand trifles and toys for children to play with. In their train you see bearded fellows and men of thirty years of age, some dressed as children with hoods and bibs, some as nurses who care for them, while the bearded babies cry after playthings or amuse themselves with spinning tops or sounding little trumpets … The Greek fur-makers of the market place of Mahmut Pasha form a separate procession, with caps of bear-skin and breeches of fur. Some are dressed from head to foot in lion's, leopard's and wolves' skins, with kalpaks of sable on their heads.

The Sultan decided that the Sugar-bakers should go first,

to the great annoyance of the Fish Cooks, who appealed to their patron Jonah and blamed the Helvacis, who reproached the Fish Cooks, saying fish was very unwholesome and infatuating food.

An Ottoman Traveller: Selections from the Book of Travels of Evliya Çelebi
(Eland Books, London, 2010)

The procession at Engelberg, 15th August, 1825
DOROTHY WORDSWORTH

… Soon after breakfast we were warned to expect the procession, and saw it issuing from the church. Priests in their white robes, choristers, monks chanting the service, banners uplifted, and a full-dressed image of the Virgin carried aloft. The people were divided into several classes: the men, bareheaded; the maidens, taking precedence of the married women, I suppose, because it was the festival of the Virgin.

The procession formed a beautiful stream upon the green level, winding round the church and convent. Thirteen hundred people were assembled at Engelberg, and joined in this service. The unmarried women wore straw hats, ornamented with flowers, white bodices, and crimson petticoats. The dresses of the elder people were curious. What a display of neck-chains and earrings! of silver and brocaded stomachers! Some old men had coats after the mode of the time of The Spectator , with worked seams. Boys, and even young men, wore flowers in their straw hats.

We entered the convent; but were only suffered to go up a number of staircases, and through long whitewashed galleries, hung with portraits of saints, and prints of remarkable places in Switzerland, and particularly of the vale and convent of Engelberg, with plans and charts of the mountains etc.

There are now only eighteen monks; and the abbot no longer exists: his office, I suppose, became extinct with his temporal kingdom … I strolled to the chapel, near the inn, a pretty white edifice, entered by a long flight of steps. No priest, but several young peasants, in shepherdess attire of jackets, and showy petticoats, and flowery hats, were paying their vows to the Virgin. A

He who limps is still walking.
STANISLAW J. LEC

colony of swallows had built their nests within the cupola, in the centre of the circular roof. They were flying overhead; and their voices seemed to me a harmonious accompaniment to the silent devotions of the rustics.

Journals of Dorothy Wordsworth (Macmillan & Co, London, 1897)

Accompanying the Rajah, 1870
THE RANEE MARGARET OF SARAWAK

Margaret Brooke was newly married to the British Rajah of Sarawak and they were met formally on their arrival in his – now, their – country, a country in which processions were a part of life.

The Resident, Mr Crookshank, and his wife were there to receive us together with Mr and Mrs Helms. Mr Helms was the Sarawak agent of the Borneo Company. With them were Mr St John, Treasurer of Sarawak, and several gentlemen belonging to the Rajah's staff. By far the most impressive were four Malay chiefs, members of the Rajah's government, in their long flowing silken robes and beautiful turbans. It was a scene of brightness and gaiety, the people having gone to some trouble to give a good welcome to their Rajah and their Ranee. Bunting and paper streamers were to be seen everywhere and fire-crackers were being let off in all directions. Suddenly, from out of the others stepped a thin, somewhat elderly Malay holding a huge umbrella of yellow satin which he unfurled and held over my husband's head. The Rajah then led the way, the Resident offered me his arm, the rest of the company formed themselves into a sort of procession on foot up the narrow path that led to the Residency. …. On reaching the Residency and before proceeding to luncheon, the attendant company were presented to me ….

The Rajah and Ranee went to Bintulu, their most northern possession on the coast of Sarawak. The Ranee looked out through the lattice-work of the fort's windows:

I saw a procession of moving objects which exactly resembled conically shaped tea-trays made of red, yellow, red and black

If you can walk with Kings – nor lose the common touch …
RUDYARD KIPLING, *REWARDS AND FAIRIES*

matting. Hundreds of them moved up the path towards the Fort, but how they moved I could not make out. Presently a great crowd of women arrived at the Court House, and, as usual, friendship was soon established between us. I asked them about the tea trays whose approach had so interested me.

"These are our hats, Rajah Ranee," they said. "We always wear hats like that. Would you like to have one?"

Each day there was another, smaller, procession when the Rajah went to work.

As the Rajah stepped outside the porch (of his house) Subu would unfurl the large yellow state umbrella over his head and they would set forth. Behind his Highness walked his Malay ministers in their rich robes and beautiful turbans, they too, in turn, being followed by the usual retinue of subordinate Malays. They looked to me so very Biblical, those dear, kind, grave Hadjis, as they marched along with their slow and stately tread. I used to feel as though I had just taken leave of Abraham or Jacob or Esau!

My Life in Sarawak (Methuen, London, 1913)

In Baden-Baden, 1880
MARK TWAIN

Not everyone who walks can step out freely and fast – some are hampered in how they can walk...

Baden-Baden sits in the lap of the hills, and the natural and artificial beauties of the surroundings are combined effectively and charmingly. The level strip of ground which stretches through and beyond the town is laid out in handsome pleasure grounds, shaded by noble trees and adorned at intervals with lofty and sparkling fountain-jets. Thrice a day a fine band makes music in the public promenade before the Conversation House, and in the afternoons and evenings that locality is populous with fashionably dressed people of both sexes, who march back and forth past the great music stand and look very much bored, though they make a show of feeling otherwise. It seems like a rather aimless and stupid existence. A good many of these people are there for a

PROCESSIONS & MARCHES

People think I have an interesting walk.
Hell, I'm just trying to hold my gut in.
ROBERT MITCHUM

real purpose, however; they are racked with rheumatism, and they are there to stew it out in hot baths. These invalids looked melancholy enough, limping about on their canes and crutches, and apparently brooding over all sorts of cheerless things. People say that Germany, with her damp stone houses, is the home of rheumatism. If that is so, Providence must have foreseen that it would be so, and therefore filled the land with the healing baths. Perhaps no other country is so generously supplied with medicinal springs as Germany.

A Tramp Abroad (American Publishing Co, 1880)

Preparing for the Coronation Procession, 1952
'AMELIA'

As far back as January when I first started taking my early morning walks through the park, I thought that the Achilles Statue at the Hyde Park Corner end of the Carriage Drive was a good place to see the Coronation Procession. So I got Peter to send down a sleeping bag from Glazeley and I stacked a bag with Aspirin, Marmite sandwiches, choc biscuits, Primula cheese, Ryvita, large, easy-fitting shoes, and an extra pair of stockings. When I left the office at 5 p.m. last night it was pouring, so I thought it would be silly to sleep out and sadly prepared to make my middle-aged way homewards. (Her brother suggested they went to a theatre and out to dinner instead) … then we walked down the Carriage Drive at about 8:45 p.m. and at the Achilles Statue there was still room, and it wasn't raining and everyone looked so cheerful that my years slipped from me and, confirming Peter's long-held opinion that I am crazy, I decided to stay the night and be blowed to the weather and a rheumatic future. He nobly struggled back to Baker Street and brought me the sleeping bag and an inflatable pillow of his own.

So here I am, at 9 a.m. on Coronation Day after a night filled with alarms, other people's excursions, and lots of rain. My bag is clammy. I've been broad awake (interrupted by rain) since 5 a.m. and it is just 10:30. The Queen has just left the Palace and of course those who are interested will be hearing the very same

PROCESSIONS & MARCHES

If you want to find out about a man,
go for a long tramp with him.
STEPHEN GRAHAM *THE GENTLE ART OF TRAMPING*

words that we are hearing so there is no need for me to comment further on that.

☆ ☆ ☆

Of course we cheered wildly:
1. Municipal dustcarts
2. Small speckled dog of unknown breed
3. Runner in singlet and pale blue shorts escorted by police on motor bikes. Who and what could he have been?

At five o'clock news of the conquest of Everest came through by 'grape vine' or jungle drums …

Co-operative Correspondence Club Magazine (CCC, 1952) reproduced in *Can Any Mother Help Me?* by Jenna Bailey (Faber & Faber, London, 2007)

The Lord Mayor's Show, 1662
WILLIAM SCHELLINKS

The order of procession was as follows:
First came all the apprentices or young trainees of the Bridewell Hospital, shoemakers, weavers, tailors and all kinds of crafts, dressed in blue with grey hoods, each with their master, walking in pairs, There followed a large number of old men and women, living on the charity of Lady Ramsey*, with red caps and blue coats, with the letters MR sewn to their dress. Then came a large number of young children, boys and girls, in twos and twos, who are brought up and educated at Christ's Hospital, all dressed in blue coats and yellow undergowns; the boys all have belts round the middle and peaked caps on their heads. … Then followed four surgeons from the Hospital with green and white sashes round their bodies, with the arms of the guild embroidered on them, with white staves in their hands. After that came a large number of governors of the (city) hospitals. Then came the trumpeters playing. Then a large number of officials on foot. Then the City Marshall of London on horseback by the side of the old Lord Mayor. … *Other people followed: sergeants, clerks, and attendants of the Court of the Lord Mayor, walking in twos. Then came the mace bearers with the sword bearer.*

Now shall I walk or shall I ride?
'Ride,' Pleasure said; 'Walk,' Joy replied.
WILLIAM HENRY DAVIES

Then followed the Lord Mayor on his richly bedecked horse, wearing a red tabard with his precious jewel hanging on a rich golden chain on his chest …

* Lady Ramsey, wife of the Lord Mayor for 1577, had left endowments to charities.

The Journal of William Schellinks' Travels in England, 1661-1663
(Royal Historical Society, London, 1993)

The Lord Mayor's Show, 1930
CHIANG YEE

Once I saw the Lord Mayor's Show by chance near Moorgate tube station. The rain was becoming gradually heavier and heavier. Nothing could be seen clearly in the procession, because most of the people in it were covered with canopies to protect them from the rain. Sometimes my view was completely shut out by the umbrellas of the people who stood in front, and I heard many complaints from other people too. Then I moved back behind the line of spectators and tried to look at the countless umbrellas. When I found a stand in the door-step of a big building I saw many umbrellas on the other side of the road too. As soon as the procession had passed by, the people on both sides suddenly joined together and swirled into a great tide in the middle of the road. I could not help crying out to myself, "Oh, umbrellas of London!" It was really a fine exhibition of umbrellas!

The Silent Traveller in London (Country Life, London, 1938; rpt Signal Books, 2001)

Beating the Bounds, 1939
H.V. MORTON

Every three years, on Ascension Day, or during Rogation Week, the Yeoman Gaoler of the Tower walks out into the streets of London with the axe over his shoulder.

Behind, two by two, march the Warders of the Tower in their full-dress uniform: scarlet tunics, breeches, red stockings, Tudor bonnets, and shoes with tri-coloured rosettes on the toes. Each man carries a halberd.

The pay is good and I can walk to work.
JOHN F. KENNEDY

The carters, who are held up to allow this strange procession to pass, become extremely witty and historical at the expense of the Wardens, sometimes leaning from high perches to shout questions about Henry VIII and Anne Boleyn.

Behind the Warders walk all the resident children of the Tower of London; and there are a surprising number of them in the married quarters. They are given a school holiday on this popular day, and they walk, holding peeled willow wands, which are handed out to each boy and girl before the procession is formed.

This ceremony is the ancient Beating the Bounds of the Tower Liberties, and it is the ghost of England that existed long before the Tower of London. The custom of beating the bounds is mentioned in the laws of Alfred the Great and Athelstan.

Led by the Chief Yeoman Warder carrying the Tower Mace, the procession marches up to Tower Hill. It halts before a warehouse wall, on which one of the boundary marks is visible.

"Now, whip it, boys, whip it!" orders the Chief Warder; and a number of boys advance on the stone and set about it with their willow switches.

The procession marches on, beating a stone opposite the Royal Mint, to the Thames, below Tower Bridge, and, with other stops – to the last boundary stones under Tower Bridge.

H.V. Morton's London (Methuen, London, 1941)

Wonderland, 1865
LEWIS CARROLL

One of the classic processions is described in Alice's Adventures in Wonderland. *Alice was talking in a garden with three gardeners. At the sound of many footsteps, Alice looked round …*

First came ten soldiers carrying clubs: these were all shaped like the three gardeners, oblong and flat, with their hands and feet at the corners: next the ten courtiers; these were ornamented all over with diamonds, and walked two and two, as the soldiers

PROCESSIONS & MARCHES

Backpacking is an extended form of hiking in which people carry double the amount of gear they need for half the

did. After these came the royal children; there were ten of them, and the little dears came jumping merrily along, hand in hand, in couples: they were all ornamented with hearts. Next came the guests, mostly Kings and Queens, and among them Alice recognised the White Rabbit: it was talking in a hurried nervous manner, smiling at everything that was said, and went by without noticing her. Then followed the Knave of Hearts, carrying the King's crown on a crimson velvet cushion; and, last of all this grand procession, came THE KING AND QUEEN OF HEARTS.

Alice was rather doubtful whether she ought not to lie down on her face like the three gardeners, but she could not remember ever having heard of such a rule at processions; "and besides, what would be the use of a procession," thought she, "if people had all to lie down on their faces, so that they couldn't see it?" So she stood where she was and waited.

Alice's Adventures in Wonderland (Macmillan & Co, London, 1865)

Procession in Marseilles, 1850
W.H. BARTLETT

I repaired to Marseilles, and took passage for Syria in the French government steamer *Osiris*. The evening before we left the city occurred one of the most striking processions ever witnessed, especially when its object is taken into account. It was a commemoration of the day on which the last fearful visitation of the plague terminated – a visitation deeply engraved in the memory of the Marseillais. It occurred about a century ago, and cut off a large portion of the population. A picture in the town records the scenes of horror when witnessed, reminding us of those vividly described by Defoe. The day, like all in this southern clime, was resplendently brilliant; the ships in the harbour were decorated with streamers; the principal shops were closed, and the whole population devoted to the enjoyment, and the religious observances of the festival. There is something contagious in the cheerfulness of one of these southern *festas*, in which all classes alike pause from their labours, and appear thoroughly to enjoy

PROCESSIONS & MARCHES

distance they planned to go in twice the time it should take.

ANON

themselves, without that riot and turbulence so common in an English holiday.

As evening drew near, the booming of the cannon over the city indicated that the procession was about to commence. The balconies along the line were decorated with carpets or festoons of bright coloured drapery, and filled with gaily dressed spectators; while those in the streets were either seated in chairs let out for the occasion, or ranged quietly along the causeway, without any of that crushing so indispensable to the enjoyment of a London mob, even when consisting of well dressed ladies and gentlemen. From the window of the hotel, near the corner of the Canebiere, I enjoyed a perfect view of the procession. It opened as usual with a number of priests bearing crucifixes and banners, often very beautifully decorated. After these came a long line of young gentlemen, smartly dressed in white trowsers and blue coats. But the most pleasing and graceful feature was the next, – an immense number of beautiful young girls, dressed in white muslin, with their hair enwreathed with chaplets of roses, sustaining silken banners inwrought with pictures of the Virgin relieving sufferers from the plague, and other appropriate subjects. Next followed a long double file of women, dressed in grey as penitents; their eyes alone were visible through the opening of their hoods, and they carried candles in their hands.

This lengthened procession which must have numbered many thousands, chanting low and solemn hymns as they filed slowly past on both sides of the road, had something inexpressibly striking, associated as it could not fail to be with the terrible incidents of the plague. An immense number of male penitents, similarly habited, kept up the endless succession, intermingled at intervals with parties of ecclesiastics, singing and bearing crosses.

By this time it had become quite dark, and the candles carried by the penitents were lighted, and, with numerous splendid silver lamps, borne by the chanting priests, gleamed through the streets with a singularly impressive effect. The heavy tread of a long file of soldiers, and the spirit-stirring strains of military music, contrasting with the sacred and solemn harmonies of the penitents and priests, which had previously been heard, brought

**These boots are made for walkin'
And that's just what they'll do...**
NANCY SINATRA, *THESE BOOTS ARE MADE FOR WALKIN'*

to a close the most affecting procession it had ever been my chance to witness.

Jerusalem Revisited, (A. Hall, Virtue & Co, London, 1855)

Ants marching in the Amazon forest, 1863
HENRY WALTER BATES

Few creatures are said 'to march' – other than ants …

Eciton praedator – This is a small, reddish species, very similar to the common red stinging-ant of England. It differs from all other Ecitons in its habit of hunting, not in columns, but in dense phalanxes consisting of myriads of individuals, and was first met with at Ega, where it is very common. Nothing in insect movements is more striking than the rapid march of these large and compact bodies. Wherever they pass all the rest of the animal world is thrown into a state of alarm. They stream along the ground and climb to the summits of all the lower trees, searching every leaf to its apex, and whenever they encounter a mass of decaying vegetable matter, where booty is plentiful, they concentrate, like other Ecitons, all their forces upon it, the dense phalanx of shining and quickly-moving bodies, as it spreads over the surface, looking like a flood of dark-red liquid. They soon penetrate every part of the confused heap, and then, gathering together again in marching order, onward they move. All soft-bodied and inactive insects fall an easy prey to them, and, like other Ecitons, they tear their victims in pieces for facility of carriage. A phalanx of this species, when passing over a tract of smooth ground, occupies a space of from four to six square yards; on examining the ants closely they are seen to move, not altogether in one straightforward direction, but in variously spreading contiguous columns, now separating a little from the general mass, now re-uniting with it. The margins of the phalanx spread out at times like a cloud of skirmishers from the flanks of an army. I was never able to find the hive of this species.

The Naturalist on the River Amazons (John Murray, London, 1863)

PROCESSIONS & MARCHES

When I see people on the street, I look at how they walk. It's like a signature, a fingerprint.
MIKHAIL BARYSHNIKOV

4

PILGRIMAGES & WALKING FOR WORK

First days in Jerusalem, 1855
ADAM STEINMETZ KENNARD

There are many accounts by walkers of pilgrimage and of walking in the Holy Land, as here.

By the time we reached our hotel we had visited, if Giuseppe was to be believed, pretty nearly all the places with the exception of those beneath the roof of the church of the Holy Sepulchre, mentioned in the New Testament. It almost seemed as if, in the grouping of them so closely together, the convenience of succeeding generations had been studied; for instance, pausing in one part of the Via Dolorosa, our guide, clearing his throat, said, "You see this building, Sir? This was the palace of Herod! This is where St Peter made his denial! – that (pointing with his finger to a spot a few yards in advance) is where the cock crew! – this house belonged to Santa Veronica, who offered the napkin – now shown at Rome on Good Fridays – to our Lord as he passed on his way to Calvary! – and just there, Sir, is where Simon the Cyrenian was compelled to bear the cross!"

A few steps further on he drew our attention to two very antiquated buildings, and astonished us by asserting that the one on the left belonged to Lazarus, whilst the other, on which still remained traces of red paint, had been the residence of Dives; and for the first time in our lives, we perceived that the beggar had been equally well lodged with his wealthy neighbour....

☆ ☆ ☆

In all my walks around Jerusalem, I found no spot so pretty as Enrogel. Surrounded with foliage and corn-fields, one forgets the sterility and desolation by which, on all other sides, the Holy City is characterized; and often, during my sojourn of three weeks here, I whiled away many a pleasant hour with my sketch-book and pencil, listening to the soporific dripping of the water from the moist sides of the well. And it is those quiet solitudes, more than all the churches and altars that are erected over the most sacred spots, and with which the city itself teems, that form the great charm to the traveller, who really visits Jerusalem with a view to bringing home to his mind the deeply-interesting fact of being where our Saviour spent the greater part of his life.

However careless a man may be of that which concerns his soul, when he leaves the noise and bustle of the city, and descends to Enrogel, or climbs the side of the Mount of Olives, or wanders forth on the road to Bethany, with the same scene before him upon which our Saviour must so often have gazed, it is impossible that such moments as these must not have their effect upon him, and make him think seriously, whether he is a believer in Christianity or not.

Continuing my walk, I left Enrogel, and climbed to the summit of the so-called Mount of the Prophets; and, gaining from thence the Mount of Olives, I once more looked upon the Holy City as the sun was commending to set, gilding with its rays the multitude of mosques and minarets which tapered up into the evening sky within its walls.

Eastern Experiences (Longmans, London, 1855)

Pilgrims met en route, 1794
J.B.S. MORRITT

En route to Constantinople Morritt passed through the Austro-Hungarian Empire and encountered pilgrims – who were regarded with a cynical Protestant eye…

At and near Maria-Zell we met quantities of pilgrims, and processions with banners, crosses, saints, and Heaven knows what to amuse them on their journey to and from the chapel. The Virgin here is in very great repute, and receives visits from the very first

When you walk ten hours, eleven hours a day by yourself, you are doing a walking meditation.
SHIRLEY MACLAINE

company, both at Vienna and still greater distances; however, when we saw her, her Court was rather numerous than brilliantly attended. She is a fat, chubby, black figure, in a massy silver shrine. Round this are people, as at Loretto, walking about on their knees. We saw a procession (which consisted of some five hundred of all ages, both men and women) make their entrée; two leading troops were crowned with little green wax crowns, just on the middle of their head. They chanted in turns something we of course did not understand, made the tour of the church once, then went in, all kissing the top step, which must, of course, be very pleasant to those that came in last – made their obeisance to different saints , and then assembled, singing in the three aisles before the shrine, which they address individually afterwards, some on their knees with tapers, some on their faces, some walking on their knees; on short, I think almost every way but walking on their heads, which I can't say I saw practised.

The Letters of John B.S. Morritt of Rokeby (Cambridge University Press, 1914)

Towards Santiago, 1843 and 2007
GUY ARNOLD AND GEORGE BORROW

Guy Arnold followed George Borrow's journey through Spain. Here, Borrow descended to the valley bottom and became enmeshed in a bog and was obliged to seek the highway on the hillside again.

We now began to descend the valley by a broad and excellent *carretera* or carriage-road, which was cut out of the steep side of the mountain on our right.

On our left was the gorge … The road was tortuous, and at every turn the scene became more picturesque. The gorge gradually widened, and the brook at its bottom increased in volume and sound, but it was soon far beneath us, pursuing its headlong course till it reached level ground, here it flowed in the midst of a beautiful but confined prairie. There was something sylvan and savage in the mountains on the farther side, clad from foot to pinnacle with trees, so closely growing that the eye was unable to obtain a glimpse of the hillsides, which were uneven with ravines

We don't think about pilgrimage in this country. We don't think about meditation. The idea of taking a six-week walk

and gulleys, the haunts of the wolf, the wild boar, and the corso, or mountain stag.

When Arnold passed this way much had changed.

This splendid description of wilderness no longer holds, for half the bottom of the valley has been turned into a vast slate quarry, and as I walked along the hillside high above the valley floor the drone of great trucks came up to me from below where they strained in slow motion, huge latter-day prehistoric monsters with their loads. The sylvan savagery that impressed Borrow has been replaced by the modern savagery of industrial exploitation …

In the Footsteps of George Borrow: A journey through Spain and Portugal
(Signal Books, Oxford, 2007) and *The Bible in Spain* (John Murray, London, 1843)

A spectral cavalcade, 1864
VISCOUNT MILTON AND DR CHEADLE

The Canadian winters on the prairies were hard for the Indians when no buffalo could be found …

During the day family after family came in – a spectral cavalcade: the men, gaunt and wan, marching before skeleton dogs, almost literally skin and bone, with hide drawn tightly and unpadded over "crate and basket, ribs and spine"; dragging painfully along sleighs as attenuated and empty of provisions as themselves. The women and children brought up the rear, who, to the credit of the men, be it recorded, were in far better case – indeed, tolerably plump, and contrasting strangely with the fleshless forms of the other sex. Although the Indian squaws and children are kept in subjection, and the work falls principally upon them, it is erroneous to suppose that they are ill-treated, or that the women labour harder or endure greater hardships than the men.

The Indian is constantly engaged in hunting, to supply his family with food; and when that is scarce, he will set out without any provision himself, and often travel from morning to night for

PILGRIMAGES & WORK

days before he finds the game he seeks; then, loaded with meat, he toils home again, and whilst the plenty lasts, considers himself entitled to complete rest after his exertions.

The North-West Passage by Land (Cassell, London, 1865)

Through New Zealand, 1773
CAPTAIN JAMES COOK

Having found some natives unfriendly, Cook determined to face them on his terms – and recorded the occasion with his idiosyncratic spelling and punctuation.

Accordingly we landed 48 Men including my self, Mr F, and officers, the Chief join'd us with a few people and we set out on our march in good order, the Chief's party gathered like a snowball as we marched thro' the Country, some arm'd and some not; Odiddy who was with us began to be alarm'd and told us that many of the people in our company were of the party we were going against and at last told us that they were only leading us to some place where they could attack us to advantage, whether there was any truth in this or only occasioned by Odiddies fears I will not pretend to say, he was however the only person we could confide in and we regulated our march accordingly; after we had march'd several miles we got intelligence that the people we were going against were fled to the Mountains, but I think we were not told this till I had declar'd to the Chief that I would March no farther for we were then about crossing a deep Vally bounded on each side with Steep Rocks where a few men with stones only might have cut off our retreat supposing their intention to be what Odiddy had said and what he still abided by; having therefore no business to proceed farther we return'd back in the same order as we went, and saw in several places people come down from the sides of the hills with their arms in their hands, which they laid down whenever they found they were seen by us, this shews that there must have been some truth in what Odiddy had said, but I must acquit Oree the Chief from having any hand in it. In our return Stoping at a house to refresh

Walking . . . is how the body measures itself against the earth.
REBECCA SOLNIT, *WANDERLUST: A HISTORY OF WALKING*

our selves with Cocoa-nutts two Chiefs brought each of them a pig and a dog and together with some young plantain trees by way of making and ratifying the Peace, after this we continued on our march to the landing place where we imbarqued and went on board …

The Journals of Captain Cook, 1768-79 (Strahan & Cadell, London, 1773)

A pilgrimage in Moscow, 1938
PETER FRANCIS

Lenin himself lies embalmed near by the Kremlin in Red Square; I took an early opportunity of going to see him. He lies*, since his death in 1924, in a simple but dignified granite mausoleum which is open from five till seven each day; even in the very bitterest weather I always saw a queue waiting to file past and pay their homage to the man whom the Russian people regard as having done more than any other to lay the foundations of their present happiness and future prosperity.

Joining the queue, which stretched shakily for some three hundred yards across Red Square, I walked slowly along till I reached the mausoleum in about fifteen minutes. In times of crisis the queue is longer. At the entrance I passed between a pair of soldiers throwing watchful glances over the slowly moving column. They are careful about hidden arms ever since the day when a German engineer tried to smash the plate-glass coffin with a hammer.

There were thermometers on the walls, as the temperature has to be kept constant. It is for this reason that the tomb can only be open for two hours a day.

Descending into the vault itself, we filed slowly round three sides of the plate-glass coffin where Nikolai Lenin lies, dressed in a greyish military uniform with just his head and shoulders showing. His hands are lying by his sides, the crossed ecclesiastical position having been carefully avoided. Over his feet lies the original flag of the 1870 Paris Commune.

There is something magnetic in that pale, waxy face and domed, intellectual forehead. Every eye was devoutly fixed on

'Solvitur ambulando', St. Augustine said.
'It is solved by walking'.
LAURA KELLY, *DISPATCHES FROM THE REPUBLIC OF OTHERNESS*

those immobile features. If the guard had not stopped them, many of those worshippers would have walked blindly on, straight into the opposite wall. I came out into the wintry sunshine, feeling that I had seen, for the first time, a simple, devout people paying their homage to the man they revered.

* Lenin still lies there today, and people queue up to walk past with interest and reverence.

I worked in a Soviet Factory (Jarrolds, London, 1938)

Marching with banners, 1860
BAYARD TAYLOR

We descended into the square, broke through the guarded space, and took leave of our maidens at the door of the council hall, where ninety-seven others were waiting for them. On all sides waved the flags of the various German States – the black and white of Prussia; blue and silver of Bavaria; red and yellow of Baden; fortress in a red field of Hamburg the Saxon and Thuringian colours; the tricolour of Schleswig-Holstein; the cross of Switzerland – and, over all, the symbol of strength and unity, the red, black and gold. What was my delight, at seeing from the corner of the square, the stars and stripes of America! Singularly enough, the only foreign power thus represented. Every house was hung with garlands – principally of German oak, looped up with knots of roses, and disposed in the infinite variety of forms, but in every instance with excellent taste. The general effect was exceedingly beautiful.

The streets through which the procession was to pass, were similarly decorated. Occasionally the wreaths were of fir, with gilded cones as pendants, or with rosettes of forget-me-knots and harebells.

At Home and Abroad: A Sketchbook of Life, Scenery and Men
(George P Putnam, New York, 1860)

I've taken to long-distance walking as a means of dissolving the mechanised matrix which compresses the space-time continuum, and decouples human from physical geography.

Tread mills, 1827
THE TIMES REPORTED IN THE TABLE BOOK

This form of 'walking' is a punishment rather than having any sort of pleasure ... Both the fact that this punishment was so carefully detailed and so varied from one place to another and by season is surprising today ...

At Lewes, in Sussex, each prisoner walks at the rate of 6,600 feet in ascent a day; at Ipswich, 7450; at St Alban's, 8000; at Bury, 8650, at Cambridge 10,176, at Durham, 12,000, at Brixton, Guildford and Reading, the summer rate exceeds 13,000; while at Warwick, the summer rate is about 17,000 feet in ten hours.

The Table Book (William Hone, London, 1827)

Through Spanish fields, 1937
GEORGE ORWELL

Serving in the Republican army during the Spanish Civil War, Orwell saw a Spain almost impossible to imagine today.

Men in ragged blue shirts and black corduroy breeches, with broad-brimmed straw hats, were ploughing the fields behind teams of mules with rhythmically flopping ears. Their ploughs were wretched things, only stirring the soil, not cutting anything we should regard as a furrow. All the agricultural implements were pitifully antiquated, everything being governed by the expensiveness of metal. A broken ploughshare, for instance, was patched, and then patched again, till sometimes it was mainly patches. Rakes and pitchforks were made of wood. Spades, among a people who seldom possessed boots, were unknown; they did their digging with a clumsy hoe like those used in India. There was a kind of harrow that took one straight back to the later Stone Age. It was made of boards joined together, to about the size of a kitchen table; in the boards hundreds of holes were morticed, and into each hole was jammed a piece of flint which had been chipped into shape exactly as men used to chip them ten thousand years ago. I remember my feeling almost of horror

So this isn't walking for leisure — that would be merely frivolous, or even for exercise — which would be tedious ....
WILL SELF, *PSYCHOGEOGRAPHY*

when I first came upon one of these things in a derelict hut in no-man's-land. I had to puzzle over it for a long while before grasping that it was a harrow. It made me sick to think of the work that must go into the making of such a thing, and the poverty that was obliged to use flint in place of steel. I have felt more kindly towards industrialism ever since. But in the village there were two up-to-date farm tractors, no doubt seized from some landowner's estate.

Once or twice I wandered out to the little walled graveyard that stood a mile or so from the village. The dead from the front were normally sent to Siétamo; these were the village dead. It was queerly different from an English graveyard. No reverence for the dead here! Everything overgrown with bushes and coarse grass, human bones littered everywhere. But the really surprising thing was the almost complete lack of religious inscriptions on the gravestones, though they all dated from before the revolution. Only once, I think, I saw the 'Pray for the soul of so-and-so' which is usual on Catholic graves. Most of the inscriptions were purely secular, with ludicrous poems about the virtues of the deceased. On perhaps one grave in four or five there was a small cross or a perfunctory reference to Heaven; this had usually been chipped off by some industrious atheist with a chisel.

Homage to Catalonia (Secker and Warburg, London, 1938)

Even when I am writing I usually take a break around lunchtime and go for a little walk to clear out my head.
PATRICIA CORNWELL

Walking on snowy days is very different from the easy enjoyment of walking on a spring afternoon or a summer morning. But there are special pleasures ...

South up the Rhine – to the Danube, 1970
PATRICK LEIGH FERMOR

The scene was beginning to change. My path followed a frozen woodland stream into a region where rushes and waterweed and marsh vegetation and brambles and shrubs were as densely entangled as a primeval forest. Opening on expanses of feathered ice, it was like a mangrove swamp in the Arctic Circle. Encased in ice and snow, every twig sparkled. Frost had turned the rushes into palisades of brittle rods and the thickets were loaded with icicles and frozen rainbow-shooting drops. Of birds, I could only see the usual crows and rooks and magpies, but the snow was arrowed with forked prints. It must have teemed with water-fowl at a different time of year and with fish too. Nets were looped stiffly in the branches and a flat-bottomed boat, three-quarters sunk, was frozen in for the winter. It was a white, hushed region under a spell of catalepsy.

It was a marvellous place; an unusual place; I couldn't quite make it out – half mere, half frozen jungle. It finished at a bank where a row of poplars was interspersed with aspen and birch and willow among blackberry-thickets, and hazel. On the other side of this barrier the sky suddenly widened and a great volume of water was flowing dark and fast. In midstream, cloudy with the hemispherical ghosts of weeping-willows, an island divided the rush of the current. There was an answering line of ice on the other bank, then reeds and woods and a fluctuation of timbered mountain.

The second meeting with the Danube had taken me unawares; I had reached it half a day sooner than I thought! As it streamed through those wooded and snowbound ranges the river made an overpowering impression of urgency and force.

My map, when I dug it out, said that the mountains opposite were part of the Bohemian Forest. They had followed the north bank ever since the river had entered Austria a mile or two east of Passau, about thirty miles upstream.

A Time of Gifts: On Foot to Constantinople (John Murray, London, 1977)

January 7th, 1773
GILBERT WHITE

Snow driving all the day, which was followed by frost, sleet, and some snow, till the 12th, when a prodigious mass overwhelmed all the works of men, drifting over the tops of the gates and filling the hollow lanes.

On the 14th the writer was obliged to be much abroad; and thinks he never before or since has encountered such rugged Siberian weather. Many of the narrow roads were now filled above the tops of the hedges; through which the snow was driven into most romantic and grotesque shapes, so striking to the imagination as not to be seen without wonder and pleasure. The poultry dared not to stir out of their roosting places; for cocks and hens are so dazzled and confounded by the glare of snow that they would soon perish without assistance. The hares also lay sullenly in their seats, and would not move until compelled by hunger; being conscious, poor animals, that the drifts and heaps treacherously betray their footprints, and prove fatal to numbers of them.

The Natural History of Selborne (T. Bensley for B. White and Son, London, 1789)

I frequently tramped eight or ten miles through the deepest snow to keep an appointment with a beech-tree,

Marching through the Antarctic, 1914
ERNEST SHACKLETON

Cutting steps with the adze, we moved in a lateral direction round the base of the dolomite, which blocked our view to the north. The same precipice confronted us. Away to the north-east there appeared to be a snow slope that might give a path to the lower country, and so we retraced our steps down the long slope that had taken us three hours to climb. We were at the bottom in an hour. We were now feeling the strain of the unaccustomed marching. We had done little walking since January and our muscles were out of tune. Skirting the base of the mountain above us, we came to a gigantic bergschrund, a mile and a half long and 1000 feet deep. This tremendous gully, cut in the snow and ice by the fierce winds blowing round the mountain, was semi-circular in form, and it ended in a gentle incline. We passed through it, under the towering precipice of ice, and at the far end we had another meal and a short rest. This was at 12:30 p.m. Half a pot of steaming Bovril ration warmed us up, and when we marched again ice-inclines at angles of 45 degrees did not look quite as formidable as before.

Once more we started for the crest …

South: The story of Shackleton's last expedition, 1914-1917
(Heinemann, London, 1919)

Winter walk on Port Meadow, Oxford, 1942
CHIANG YEE

Chiang Yee, a student at Oxford, heard one winter morning the hungry cheep of a bird outside his window. He resolved to share a little of his breakfast…

I came to Kingston Road, where a great roaring and shouting greeted me. A snow fight was in progress, the boys being divided into two groups. Some had got hold of dustbin lids and were using them as shields like warriors of old. It was a comical sight.

or a yellow birch, or an old acquaintance among the pines.
H.D. THOREAU

Though walking slowly, my feet trod lightly on the snow, and it did not take me long to get to Port Meadow by way of Aristotle Lane. There I stopped to admire some rugged willows of great beauty, whose myriad slender branches and elegant twigs intermingled in intricate patterns. Suddenly a small shower of white powder fell, or rather was shaken, from one of the lower thicker branches.

I looked up in surprise, for there was at that moment neither wind nor snowfall. It was a redbreast, that daring and sociable creature, hopping from branch to branch and chirping as if for food. I remembered my errand, and threw some breadcrumbs.

Birds arrived with extraordinary speed ... I left them gobbling the remnants of their feast.

Standing at the edge of the Meadow, I looked at the vast flat stretch of whiteness whose cold purity brought peace to the heart. So much snow had fallen that the low meadow had been raised to the level of the footpath, which is slightly higher. It seemed that the earth had been lifted closer to the sky, its surface broadened, and distant objects brought into clearer view. I could distinctly see the little village of Binsey, and Wytham Hill too, usually hidden by tall trees on the river-bank behind. Yet everything was in miniature: the trees, the village houses, and Wytham Hill, though sharp in outline, resembled a miniature bas-relief, as did the village of Wolvercote.

A man and a dog were coming towards me, apparently without legs, for the stillness and the soft atmosphere, with the low-hanging grey sky, seemed to deny all movement.

From my left, nearby, came the clamour of skaters, and I watched them for a while. Far beyond I saw the slender tower of St Barnabas, piercing the sky. Then by way of Willow Walk I reached the snow laden wooden bridge. The Thames was not frozen and the water flowed steadily, dark against the snowy banks, where in warm weather it had gleamed against the darker grass. What infinite variety the seasons give!

The Silent Traveller in Oxford (Methuen, London 1944; rpt Signal Books, Oxford 2001)

A bear, however hard he tries, grows tubby without exercise. A.A. MILNE, *WINNIE-THE-POOH*

Animals in the snow, 1888
C.J. CORNISH

Walking across the fields after a violent snow-storm in January, the writer stepped on a hare, though the field showed one level stretch of driven snow; and, later in the day, from the brow of a steep, narrow valley, the sun-holes made by the hares were easily marked on the opposite ridge. ... Squirrels, which are often supposed to hibernate, only retire to their nests in very severe and prolonged frosts. A slight fall of snow only amuses them, and they will come down from their trees and scamper over the powdery heaps with immense enjoyment. What they do not like is the snow on the leaves and branches, which falls in showers as they jump from tree to tree, and betrays them to their enemies, the country boys.

Like the squirrels, rabbits seem to rather enjoy the snow at first. Like many men, they require a dry, bracing atmosphere, and sea-breezes and frost suit them; and the morning after a snow-fall their tracks show where they have been scratching and playing in it all night. But after a deep fall they are soon in danger of starving. Though not particular as to quality, they like their meals 'reg'lar', and with all the grass covered with a foot of snow their main supply of food is cut off. If there is a turnip-field near, they will scratch away the snow to the roots, and soon destroy the crop. If not, or if the surface of the snow is frozen hard, the hungry bunnies strip the bark from the trees and bushes. In the long frost of February, 1888, we saw nothing but bare white wood in the fences near the warrens. Ivy bark seemed their favourite food, and even the oldest stems were stripped, making a white network against the trunks of the big trees.

Wild England of Today and the Wildlife in it (Seeley & Co, London, 1895)

I am pushing sixty. That is enough exercise for me.
MARK TWAIN

Erzurum in the Armenian winter, 1854
ROBERT CURZON

Very few people were about, the bulk of the population hibernating at this time of year in their strange holes and burrows. The bright colours of the Oriental dresses looked to my eyes strangely out of place in the cold dirty snow; scarlet robes, jackets embroidered with gold, brilliant green and white costumes, were associated in my mind with a hot sun, a dry climate, and fine weather. A bright sky there was, with the sun shining away as if it was all right, but his rays gave out no heat, and only put your eyes out with its glare upon the snow …

Another inconvenience has an absurd effect: the breath, out of doors, congeals upon the moustaches and beard, and speedily produces icicles, which prevent the possibility of opening the mouth. My moustaches were converted each day into two sharp icicles, and if anything came against them it hurt horribly; and those who wore long beards were often obliged to commence the series of Turkish civilities in dumb show; their faces being fixtures for the time, they were not able to talk until their beard thawed.

Armenia (John Murray, London, 1854)

Bad weather in May, 1827
DOROTHY WORDSWORTH

Friday, 14th May. A very cold morning – hail and snow showers all day. We went to Brothers Wood, intending to get plants, and to go along the edge of the lake to the foot. We did go a part of the way, but there was no pleasure in stepping along that difficult sauntering road in this uncongenial weather. We turned again and walked backwards and forwards in Brothers Wood. William tired himself with thinking of an epithet for a cuckoo. I sat a while upon my last summer seat, the mossy stone. … The oak trees are just putting forth yellow knots of leaves. The ashes with their flowers passing away, and leaves coming out; the blue hyacinth is not quite full blown; gowans are coming out; marsh marigolds in full

Some people walk in the rain, others just get wet.
ROGER MILLER

glory; the little star plant, a star without a flower. We took home a great load of gowans and planted them about the orchard.

After dinner, I worked bread, then came and mended socks beside William. He fell asleep. After tea I walked to Rydale for letters. It was a strange night. The hills were covered over with a slight covering of hail or snow, just so as to give them a hoary winter look with the black rocks. The woods looked miserable, the coppices green as grass, which looked quite unnatural, and they seemed half shrivelled up, as if they shrank from the air. O, thought I! what a beautiful thing God has made winter to be, by stripping the trees, and letting us see their shapes and forms. What a freedom it seems to give to the storms!

Journals of Dorothy Wordsworth (Macmillan & Co, London, 1897)

The end of the year, 1939
LILIAS RIDER HAGGARD

Christmas morning, and all our particular little world white and very still – buried deep in snow. Snow over hills and Common eighteen inches deep, snow weighing down the trees and piled thick on the hedges. The river covered with grey, sodden ice, with a few open stretches were swans and cygnets paddled uneasily to and fro, unable to get the twenty-yard stretch they need to rise upon the wing. We went up to the House for dinner in the evening and tramped home laden with parcels, the snow coming over the top of our gum boots. At the bottom of the hill the light shone out onto a fairy scene, reminding me of the legend that every house should put a candle in the window on Christmas night lest the passing Christ Child should lose His way. Also of the news given in a few short sentences on the wireless on Christmas Eve – that hundreds of refugees had been turned out of the stables and barns where they had sheltered, to wander in the streets and forests. Twenty centuries after the birth of Christ, men, women and children in Europe were denied even the shelter of a stable such as sheltered Him, of the company of the beasts who lay by His manger.

A Country Scrap-Book (Faber & Faber, London, 1950)

The English winter – ending in July to recommence in August. BYRON, *DON JUAN*

WALKING IN WINTER

6

ON HILLS AND MOUNTAINS

Real climbing is different from walking, but sometimes, on a walk, we must climb – and clamber.....

Meeting Thesiger in Afghanistan, 1958
ERIC NEWBY

"Look," said Hugh, "it must be Thesiger."

Coming towards us out of the great gorge where the river thundered was a small caravan like our own. He named an English explorer, a remarkable throwback to the Victorian era, a fluent speaker of Arabic, a very brave man, who has twice crossed the Empty Quarter and, apart from a few weeks every year, has passed his entire life among primitive peoples.

We had been on the march for a month. We were all rather jaded; the horses were galled because the drivers were careless of them, and their ribs stood out because they had been in places only fit for mules and forded innumerable torrents filled with slippery rocks as big as footballs; the drivers had run out of tobacco and were pining for their wives; there was no more sugar to put in the tea, no more jam, no more cigarettes and I was reading *The Hound of the Baskervilles* for the third time; all of us suffered from persistent dysentery. The ecstatic sensations we had experienced at a higher altitude were beginning to wear off. It was not a particularly gay party.

Thesiger's caravan was abreast of us now, his horses lurching to a standstill on the execrable track. They were deep-loaded with great wooden presses, marked 'British Museum', and black tin trunks. The party consisted of two villainous-looking tribesmen dressed like royal mourners in long overcoats reaching to the ankles; a shivering Tajik cook, to whom some strange mutation had given bright red hair, unsuitably dressed for central Asia in crippling pointed brown shoes and natty socks supported by suspenders, but no trousers; the interpreter, a gloomy-looking middle-class Afghan in a coma of fatigue, wearing dark glasses, a double-breasted lounge suit and an American hat with stitching all over it; and Thesiger himself, a great, long-striding crag of a man, with an outcrop for a nose and bushy eyebrows, 45 years old and as hard as nails, in an old tweed jacket, a pair of thin grey cotton trousers, rope-soled Persian slippers and a woollen cap comforter. "Turn round," he said, "you'll stay the night with us. We're going to kill some chickens."

We tried to explain that we had to get to Kabul, that we wanted our mail, but our men, who professed to understand no English but were reluctant to pass through the gorges at night, had already turned the horses and were making for the collection of miserable hovels that was the nearest village. Soon we were sitting on a carpet under some mulberry trees, surrounded by the entire population, with all Thesiger's belongings piled up behind us. "Can't speak a word of the language," he said cheerfully. "Know a lot of the Koran by heart but not a word of Persian. Still, it's not really necessary. Here, you," he shouted at the cook, who had only entered his service the day before and had never seen another Englishman. "Make some green tea and a lot of chicken and rice – three chickens."

"No good bothering the interpreter," he went on, "the poor fellow's got a sty, that's why we only did 17 miles today."

Soon the cook was back, semaphoring desperately. "Speak up, can't understand a thing. You want sugar? Why don't you say so?" he produced a bunch of keys, like a housekeeper in some stately home.

"That cook's going to die," said Thesiger; "hasn't got a coat and look at his feet. We're 9,000 feet if we're an inch here. How high's the Chamar Pass?" We told him 16,000 feet. "Get yourself a coat and boots, do you hear?" he shouted in the direction of the camp fire.

After two hours the chickens arrived; they were like elastic, only the rice and gravy were delicious.

ON HILLS & MOUNTAINS

It is not the mountain we conquer but ourselves.
EDMUND HILLARY

"England's going to pot," said Thesiger, as Hugh and I lay smoking the interpreter's king-size cigarettes, the first for a fortnight. "Look at this shirt, I've only had it three years, now it's splitting. Same with tailors; Gull and Croke made me a pair of whipcord trousers to go to the Atlas Mountains. Sixteen guineas – wore a hole in them in a fortnight. Bought half a dozen shotguns to give to my headmen, well-known make, 20 guineas apiece, absolute rubbish."

He began to tell me about his Arabs. "I give them powders for worms and that sort of thing." I asked him about surgery. "I take off fingers and there's a lot of surgery to be done. They're frightened of their own doctors because they're not clean."

"Do you do it? Cutting off fingers?"

"Hundreds of them," he said dreamily, for it was very late. "Lord yes. Why, the other day I took out an eye. I enjoyed that. Let's turn in."

The ground was like iron with sharp rocks sticking up out of it. We started to blow up our air-beds. "God, you must be a couple of pansies," said Thesiger.

A Short Walk in the Hindu Kush (Secker & Warburg, London, 1958)

Starting out on an Alpine day, 1880
MARK TWAIN

Climbing the Rigi-Kulm, "an imposing Alpine mass, 6000 feet high" from a lake near its foot, Twain started upward.

We were soon tramping leisurely up the leafy mule-path, and then the talk began to flow, as usual. It was twelve o'clock noon, and a breezy, cloudless day; the ascent was gradual, and the glimpses, from under the curtaining boughs, of blue water, and tiny sail-boats, and beetling cliffs, were as charming as glimpses of dreamland. All the circumstances were perfect – and the anticipations, too, for we should soon be enjoying, for the first time, that wonderful spectacle, an Alpine sunrise – the object of our journey. There was (apparently) no real need to hurry, for the guide-book made the walking distance from Waggis to the summit only three hours and quarter. I say 'apparently', because the

My father considered a walk among the mountains as the equivalent of churchgoing. ALDOUS HUXLEY

guide book had already fooled us once – about the distance from Allerheiligen to Oppenau – and for aught I knew might be getting ready to fool us again.

A Tramp Abroad (American Publishing Co, 1880)

Climbing at Cortina, 1872
AMELIA EDWARDS

To ascend the Campanile and get the near view over the village, was obviously one of the first duties of a visitor; so, finding the door open and the old bell-ringer inside, we mounted laboriously to the top – nearly a hundred feet higher than the leaning tower of Pisa. Standing here upon the outer gallery above the level of the great bells, we had the village and valley at our feet. The panorama, though it included little which we had not seen already, was fine all round, and served to impress the main landmarks upon our memory. The Ampezzo Thal opened away to North and South, and the twin passes of the Tre Croce and Tre Sassi intersected it to East and West. When we had fixed in our minds the fact that Landro and Brunek lay out to the North, and Perarolo to the South; that Auronzo was to be found somewhere on the other side of the Tre Croce; and that to arrive at Caprile it was necessary to go over the Tre Sassi, we had gained something in the way of definite topography.

Untrodden Peaks and Unfrequented Valleys (Longman's, Green & Co, London, 1873)

Towards the Chinese temple, 1932
ANN BRIDGE

Chieh T'ai Ssu is approached from below by a paved road, winding up and round the curves and hollows of the hill, crossing the beds of torrents on beautifully-arched bridges, and protected always on the valley side, by a plastered parapet. On leaving the smallpox village, the General's little party turned to the left, crossed a stream near a broken high-backed bridge, and began the ascent of this road.

To climb steep hills requires a slow pace at first.
WILLIAM SHAKESPEARE

For the first time for nearly eight miles they walked in the shade, for they were close in under the hill now, and the ridge cut off the sun. And immediately the fruit blossom was about them. All over the brown hill-side, on narrow stone-built terraces and wherever the slope would hold a little soil, stood the trees, so irregularly and in such profusion as to suggest a natural growth – the pink of almond-flower, the deeper pink of apricot, the phlox-like greenish white of pear-blossom. But with no green carpet, pied with daisies, below them; straight from the brown soil, an incredible flowering from the still naked earth. North China, with its rainless snowless winter, knows no spring as Europe knows it – only the deep-rooted plants and trees can come to life. Later the thunder-storms of early summer revive the parched world, covering the hills with a rank un-nourishing verdure, but in spring the flowering trees carry the torch of birth alone. Unbelievable, the shock of this beauty – the delicately-shaped perfection of flower of rose and paler rose and white, against the unrelieved fawn-coloured background. It is easy, here, to see why the Chinese have painted their masterpieces of flowers on backgrounds of brown silk – even Nature, in China, is a consummate artist, and with a sure hand has shown the way in which that race of consummate artists has followed, to produce a beauty unknown to the Western world. If you want to get some idea of the road to Chieh T'ai Ssu, go to the British Museum and look at the Chinese paintings – above all at the "Earthly Paradise".

Peking Picnic (Little, Brown & Co, Boston, 1932)

The stones of Palestine, 2000
Raja Shehadeh

Normally, when I only had time for a short walk, I would continue straight down and once in the valley I would turn around and walk back up. Today I had more time. Rather than continue down, I decided to head northwards, traversing the hill I was on and going down into the next gully. The further away from town I moved the less cultivated were the fields, until I got to a hill that

Great things are done when men and mountains meet;
This is not done by jostling in the street.
WILLIAM BLAKE, *NOTEBOOKS* (1793)

was covered with weeds.Here and there, hanging down from the stone terraces I could see dead charcoal-black branches, remnants of the once vibrant grapevines that had filled these hills, cascading down over the terrace walls. I stopped to examine them. I could smell their damp rot.

Most of the rocks here are limestone, sedimentary rock formed under the deep sea that once covered these hills. I often found fossils of different shellfish. On my desk at home I have several fossilized snails. Only on this side of the Great Fault can sea fossils be found. On the east side of the River Jordan, where the shallow edge of the ancient sea was, there is only terrestrial sandstone and grit.

Nearby I noticed a number of strange-looking rocks. I knelt down to examine them more closely. Protruding out of them like a relief were tube-like fossilized roots. I picked up one of them, the size of my palm, which was embedded in the terrace wall. I noticed it because it was the colour of the brown soil, unlike the grey rocks used to build the wall. I held it in my hand and examined it closely. I was amazed. It looked as if hundreds of shells of seasnails, starfish and sea urchins had been pressed together to form this small grooved rock.

… This rock must have been millions of years old, from when this area was submerged under the sea.

Palestinian Walks: Forays into a Vanishing Landscape (Profile Books, London, 2007)

In a churchyard, 1825
DOROTHY WORDSWORTH

In a town in Germany the Wordsworths climbed to the churchyard.

A small white church, with a graceful tower, mitre-topped and surmounted by a slender spire,was in prospect, upon an eminence in the Vale, and thitherward the people led us. Passing through the small village of Engelbole, at the foot of the green eminence, we ascended to the churchyard, where was a numerous assemblage (you must not forget it was Sunday) keeping festival. It was like a fair to the eye; but no squalls of trumpets or whistles – no

ON HILLS & MOUNTAINS

Truly it may be said that the outside of a mountain is good for the inside of a man.
GEORGE WHERRY

battering of children's drums – all the people quiet, yet cheerful – cakes and fruit spread abundantly on the churchyard wall.

A beautiful prospect from that spot – new scenes to tempt us forward! We descended, by a long flight of steps, into the Vale, and, after about half a mile's walking, we arrived at Brunnen. Espied William and Mary upon a crag above the village, and they directed us to the Eagle Inn, where I instantly seated myself before a window, with a long reach of the Lake of Uri before me, the magnificent commencement to our regular approach to the St Gothard Pass of the Alps. My first feeling was of extreme delight in the excessive *beauty* of the scene: – I had expected something of a more awful impression from the Lake of Uri; but nothing so *beautiful*.

Journals of Dorothy Wordsworth (Macmillan & Co, London, 1897)

At Dendor on the Nile, 1846
HARRIET MARTINEAU

Miss Martineau was a great walker. Here, in Nubia, she strode up from the Nile to visit a temple. The Nile then, before the creation of the Aswan High Dam, was very different from the Nile today – its walls often rising steeply on either side of the river …

Of the temple of Dendor there is little to say, as it is of Roman time, and, therefore, only imitative Egyptian. It has a grotto behind, in the rock; and this grotto contained a pit; so I suppose it is a place of burial. The temple is sacred to the great holy family of Egypt, Osiris, Isis, and Horus; and the sacred chamber contains only a tablet, with a sculpture of Isis upon it, and a few hieroglyphic signs. The quantity of stones heaped in and about this little temple is remarkable.

I took a walk over the rising ground behind till I lost sight of the temple and our boat and people; and never did I see anything wilder than the whole range of the landscape. There was a black craggy ravine on either hand, which must occasionally, I should think, be the passage of torrents. There are rains now and then, however rarely, in this country; and when they do come, they are

ON HILLS & MOUNTAINS

There may be more to learn from climbing the same mountain a hundred times than by climbing a hundred different mountains. RICHARD NELSON

violent. Some of the tombs at Thebes (Luxor) bear mournful witness of the force with which torrents rush through any channels of the rocks that they can find. Not only were these ravines black, but the whole wide landscape, except a little peep of the Nile, and a bit of purple distance to the north, and two lilac summits to the south, peeping over the dark ridge. Nothing more dreary could well be conceived, unless it be an expanse of polar snow; yet it was exquisitely beautiful in point of colour – the shining black of the whole surface, except where the shadows were jet, the bright green margin of the inch of river; the white sheikh's tomb behind the palms on that tiny spot; and the glowing amethyst of the two southern summits – these in combination were soft and brilliant to a degree inconceivable to those who have not yet been in the tropics. There was a bracing mild wind on this ridge, which, by reviving the bodily sense, seem to freshen the outward world; and truly sorry I was to return. This was my last gaze upon tropical scenery too. We were to leave the tropic this afternoon, at Kalabsheh.

Eastern Life (Edward Moxon, London, 1848)

View from Fort William, 1893
MARY KINGSLEY

Sailing south down the coast of West Africa, Mary Kingsley stopped in the country we know as Ghana – then the Gold Coast.

This being done I was taken up an unmitigated hill, on whose summit stands Fort William, a pepper-pot-like structure now used as a lighthouse. Our peregrinations having been carried on under a fancy temperature, I was inclined to drink in the beauty of this building from a position at its base, and was looking round for a shady spot to sit down in, when my intentions were ruthlessly frustrated by my companions, who would stop at nothing short of its summit, where I eventually found myself. The view was exceedingly lovely and extensive. Beneath, and between us and the sea, lay the town in the blazing sun. In amongst its solid buildings patches of native mud-built huts huddled together as

ON HILLS & MOUNTAINS

It isn't the mountain ahead that wears you out;
it's the grain of sand in your shoe.
ROBERT W. SERVICE

though they had been shaken down out of a sack into the town to serve as dunnage. Then came the snow-white surf wall, and across it the blue sea with our steamer rolling to and fro on the long, regular swell, impatiently waiting until Sunday should be over and she could work cargo. Round us on all the other sides were wooded hills and valleys, and away in the distance to the west showed the white town and castle of Elmina and the nine-mile road thither, skirting the surf-bound seashore, only broken on its level way by the mouth of the Sweet River. Over all was the brooding silence of the noonday heat, broken only by the dulled thunder of the surf.

Travels in West Africa (Macmillan & Co, London, 1897)

Up the valleys, 1845
BAYARD TAYLOR

I had engaged a man to be ready in the morning to accompany me to the Bischofsgrun, ten miles further; but the man turned out to be an old woman. However, it made little difference as she walked quite as fast with her load as I was willing to walk without one. The same temperature continued; there was not a cloud in the sky, and a thin silvery shimmer of heat in the air and over the landscape. We followed the course of the young Main, at first through a wide, charming valley, whose meadows of grass and flowers fairly blazed in the sunshine, while on either hand towered the dark blue-green forests of fir. Shepherds with their flocks were on the slopes, and the little goose-girls drove their feathered herds along the road. One of them drew a wagon in which a goose and a young child were sitting cosily together. The cuckoo sang in all the woods, and no features of life failed which the landscape suggested unless it were the Tyrolean yodel. After an hour's hard walking the valley became a steep gorge, up which the road wound through continuous forests.

The scenery was now thoroughly Swiss in its character, and charmed me almost to forgetfulness of my weak and bruised knees. Still I heartily rejoiced when we reached Bischofsgrun

Earth and sky, woods and fields, lakes and rivers, the mountain and the sea, are excellent schoolmasters, and teach

(Bishop's green), a village at the base of the Ochsenkopf, one of the highest summits of the Fichtelgebirge. Here a rampant golden lion hung out, the welcome sign of food and rest.

Views A-foot, or, Europe Seen with a Knapsack and Staff
(Wiley & Putnam, New York, 1846)

To the top of the hill, Bath, 1942
Lilias Rider Haggard

Moved down to the Bath house the first of September to take joyful possession of house, and garden, and all the particular treasures whose value lies in their dear familiarity. Wet and blowy all day. After tea the rain stopped and I went up into the fields at the top of the hill. Big, lonely fields of poor light land, this year mostly cropped down with flax lying in damp brown bundles on the young green of springing plants, starred here and there with a flower blue as bird's eye. It is seldom you see a living soul up there, only the rabbits thumping and rocking leisurely off into the great wide hedges smothered in bramble and bracken, their white scuts bobbing in the dusk, pheasants rising under one's feet with thunderous wings, and a flock of plover straggling home across the sky, filling the air with the whip and whisper of their flight. I came back and stood on the brow of the hill watching a barn owl floating along the marsh, working slowly up and down his beat. It was one of those still evenings of autumn which seem to hold an illusion of spring. The pale rain-washed sky, the wet, warm smell of earth, tentative scraps of songs from the birds beginning to recover from the silence of the moult, a partridge jugging on the plough, and a couple of big bats hawking under the shelter of the wood. Only the blueness of the shadows in the hollow, and their depth beneath the sharp tilt of the barn roof jutting out against the sky line, the bright gold of new corn stacks, and the purple blackberries and scarlet hips tell a different tale. The day faded out, slowly emptying the world of light, a cold young moon sailed up over the Common, and I called the dogs and went home contentedly to supper and a wood fire.

A Country Scrap-Book (Faber & Faber, London, 1950)

ON HILLS & MOUNTAINS

some of us more than we can ever learn from books.
John Lubbock

A steep descent, 1872
AMELIA EDWARDS

… The path now turns abruptly to the left and plunges down through the steep pine forest. Somewhere among those green abysses, half-way between here and Predazzo, lies the Hospice of Paneveggio, where we are to dine and make our mid-day rest. On the verge of the dip we dismount, promising ourselves to walk so far, and leaving the men and mules to follow. It is a grand forest. The primeval pines up here are of gigantic size, rising from eighty to over a hundred feet, enormous in girth, and garlanded with hoary grey-green moss, the growth of centuries. Except only the pines close under the summit of the Wengern Alp on the Grindelwald side, I have never seen any so ancient and so majestic. As we descend they become smaller, and after the first five or six hundred feet, dwindle to the average size.

A fairly good path, cool and shady, carried down for a distance of more than 1500 feet in a series of bold zigzags, and commanding here and there grand sweeping views of forest slope and valley, brings us to an open space of green pasture, in the midst of which are clustered a wee church, a pretty white hostelry, and a group of picturesque farm-buildings. Steep hillsides of pine-woods enclose this little nest on every side. There is a pleasant sound of running water, and a tinkling of cow-bells on the air. The hay-makers on the grassy slope behind the house are singing at their work – singing what sounds like an old German chorale, in four parts. It is a delicious place; so peaceful, so pastoral, so clean, that we are almost tempted to change our plans, and stay here altogether until tomorrow.

Untrodden Peaks and Unfrequented Valleys (Longman's, Green & Co, London, 1873)

ON HILLS & MOUNTAINS

An early-morning walk is a blessing for the whole day. H.D. THOREAU

The old corpse road, 1984
ALFRED WAINWRIGHT

From the col, the path doubles back at a higher level, climbing gradually, first on grass and then amongst rock outcrops, with a sharp zigzag to reach a wall on the crest of the ridge. Looking over the wall there is a splendid full-length view of Riggindale, now without a habitation, the former farm buildings at the mouth of this wild recess having also been casualties of the flood. From this viewpoint, the rocky escarpment of Rough Crag, above which the route continues, can be seen extending into the distance; around the head of the dale is a rim of crags, and on the far side rises the peaked summit of Kidsty Pike in profile.

Looking back over The Rigg and the reservoir to the fellside beyond, the zigzags of the old corpse road can be discerned, this being the way along which the dead of Mardale Green were carried, strapped to the back of horses, for interment at Shap, eight hilly miles distant. This practice ceased in 1729 with the building of Mardale Church and the granting of a right of burial in a graveyard adjoining.*

* In early days, in remote parts of the northern Dales, where there was no church, when people died in the frozen winter months, their corpses could not be brought down from the fells to a churchyard until the weather improved.

Fellwalking with Wainwright: 18 of the author's favourite walks in Lakeland
(Michael Joseph, London, 1984)

We are indeed in Scotland, 1850
DOROTHY WORDSWORTH

Dorothy Wordsworth walked daily in the Lake District, and here her description obliquely contrasts the Scottish country with the countryside she knew best.

After ascending a little while we heard the murmur of a stream far below us, and saw it flowing downwards on our left, towards the Nith, and before us, between steep green hills, coming along

ON HILLS & MOUNTAINS

a winding valley. The simplicity of the prospect impressed us very much ....

We now felt indeed that we were in Scotland; there was a natural peculiarity in this place. In the scenes of the Nith it had not been the same as England, but yet not simple, naked Scotland. The road led us down the hill, and now there was no room in the vale but for the river and the road; we had sometimes the stream to the right; sometimes to the left. The hills were pastoral, but we did not see many sheep; green smooth turf on the left, no ferns. On the right the heath-plant grew in abundance, of the most exquisite colour; it covered a whole hillside, or it was in streams and patches. We travelled along the vale without appearing to ascend for some miles; all the reaches were beautiful, in exquisite proportion, the hills seeming very high from being so near to us. It might have seemed a valley which nature had kept to herself for pensive thoughts and tender feelings, but that we were reminded at every turning of the road of something beyond by the coal-carts which were travelling towards us.

After a time the road took us upwards towards the end of the valley. Now the steeps were healthy all round. Just as we began to climb the hill we saw three boys who came down the cleft of a brow on our left; one carried a fishing-rod, and the hats of all were braided with honeysuckles; they ran after one another as wanton as the wind. I cannot express what a character of beauty those few honeysuckles in the hats of the three boys come from? We walked up the hill, met two well-dressed travellers, the woman barefoot. Our little lads before they had gone far were joined by some half-dozen of their companions, all without shoes and stockings. They told us they lived at Wanlockhead, the village above, pointing to the top of the hill ...

When, after a steep ascent, we had reached the top of the hill, we saw a village about half a mile before us on the side of another hill, which rose up above the spot where we were, and after a descent, a sort of valley below. Nothing grew upon this ground, or the hills above or below, but heather ...

Journals of Dorothy Wordsworth (Macmillan & Co, London, 1897)

ON HILLS & MOUNTAINS

What are men to rocks and mountains?
JANE AUSTEN, *PRIDE AND PREJUDICE*

Over the moors and up the hills, 1933
CONSTANCE SITWELL

As soon as we had finished breakfast Jim and I set out for a lengthy walk over the moors and hills. It was a shining day and the landscape so gay in colour that we could scarcely believe it was the severe north country (of England) we looked upon. Stumbling over heather, pushing through bracken, following grassy tracts, we walked from nine o'clock till afternoon without any fatigue, such eager strength and freshness was breathed in the air.

Away on the horizon stretched the sea; the fields, drenched with autumn moisture, lay silvery-green far below. At last, after panting up to the top of the hill we stopped, and sitting down, surveyed the view; on all sides one could gaze and eye and mind be filled with spaciousness. At our feet cranberries were growing amongst the brown soaked stalks of bracken; the tiny cranberry leaves, turning to palest vermilion and orange, gleamed wet, and from out of them a group of belated harebells held up their lilac heads, delicate yet strong. I picked one and looked at the flawless shape.

"I never get used to the contrast between the views from mountains and hills, and the minute flowers which grow on them," I said to Jim.

"It strikes one most of all in the Himalayas, I suppose," he answered. "The rosy primulas, and the vast snowfields beyond backed by naked peaks."

"Snow and flowers! Isn't that always an exciting combination?" and I went on to the loveliest place that I remembered.

Petals and Places (Jonathan Cape, London, 1935)

ON HILLS & MOUNTAINS

I'm sure I should be myself were I once among the heather on those hills. EMILY BRONTË, *WUTHERING HEIGHTS*

7

WALKING IN PARKS AND GARDENS

In the spring when the first bulbs are in bud with the promise of flowers to come, walking is a great pleasure. Wandering in gardens or city parks or the parks of the great houses can be an adventure...

Palermo, 1787
JOHANN WOLFGANG VON GOETHE

In the public gardens, adjoining the road, I peacefully passed the most pleasurable hours. It is the most marvellous spot in the world. Laid out in regular order, it yet seems to us to be fairy-like; planted no great time since, it sets us down amidst antiquity. Green parterres embrace foreign shrubs, lemon-espoliers arch themselves into comely leaf-shaded walks, lofty walls of oleander, gemmed with a thousand red clove-like blossoms, arrest the eye. Foreign trees entirely unknown to me, still leafless, probably from warmer climes, spread forth curious branches. A bench raised behind the level ground brings into view vegetation so wonderfully, and guides the gaze at last to great basins, wherein gold and silver fish dart fascinatingly about, now hiding under mossy reeds, now assembling again in schools, lured by a bit of bread. Everywhere upon the plants appears a green that we are not used to see, now yellower, now bluer than with us. But that which threw over the whole, the rarest grace was a hazy vapour, pervading everything uniformly with so striking effect, that objects but a few steps distance behind one another, stood forth by a distinct shade of light blue from each other, so that their own colour was finally lost, or at least presented itself to the eye through a blue medium.

How wondrous a view such an atmosphere imparts to more distant objects, ships, headlands, is noteworthy enough for an artist's eye, since distances may be accurately distinguished, even measured; on which account a walk along the heights was highly charming: Nature, was no longer seen, but only pictures, as the most consummate artist might have gradated them by means of glazing.

Italian Journey 1786-1788 (Collins, London, 1962)

The Garden of Damascus, 1836
A.W. KINGLAKE

Wild as the highest woodland of a deserted home in England, but without its sweet sadness, is the sumptuous Garden of Damascus. Forest trees tall and stately enough, if you could see their lofty crests, yet lead a bustling life of it below, with their branches struggling against strong numbers of bushes and wilful shrubs. The shade upon the earth is black as night. High, high above your head, and on every side all down to the ground, the thicket is hemmed in and choked in by the interlacing boughs that droop with the weight of roses and load the slow air with their damask breath. The rose-trees which I saw were all of the kind we call damask – they grow to an immense height and size. There are no other flowers. Here and there, there are patches of ground made clear from the cover, and these are either carelessly planted with some common and useful vegetable, or else are left free to the wayward ways of nature, and bear rank weeds, moist-looking and cool to your eyes, and freshening the sense with their earthy and bitter fragrance. There is a lane opened through the thicket, so broad in some places that you can pass along side by side – in some so narrow (the shrubs are forever encroaching) that you ought, if you can, to go on the first and hold back the bough of the rose-tree. And through this wilderness there tumbles a loud rushing stream, which is halted at last in the lowest corner of the garden, and then tossed up in the fountain by the side of the simple alcove. This is all. Never for an instant will the people

Look deep into nature, and then you will understand everything better. ALBERT EINSTEIN

of Damascus attempt to separate the idea of bliss from these wild gardens and rushing waters.

Eothen; or Traces of travel brought home from the East (John Ollivier, London, 1844)

Return to England, 1933
CONSTANCE SITWELL

On the first morning after breakfast I went off by myself into the garden; the hovering breath and scent of spring was everywhere, and one could smell the box hedges and the honey-smell of berberis as one sauntered along the damp and steamy paths; I picked two bunches of small white violets which grew in the shrubbery; in the sudden heat it was pure delight to gather the violets growing frail and fragile among the roots of trees and dark ground-ivy. I went and looked at all the flowers, so satisfying in their impermanency, their freshness; they are never dusty, or remain too long, and they are never old. What a lovely background this place made for youth, I thought, and keeping the same background makes the drama which moves across in front of it more easily perceived as it changes and the years pass.

Petals and Places (Jonathan Cape, London, 1935)

Met in the rose gardens of Feddamean, 1912
LADY EVELYN COBBOLD

Lady Evelyn, having travelled through the heat and dust of Egypt, doubly welcomed the cool, lush greenness of the gardens at the end of the day.

We wander into a garden where roses looping from hibiscus to mimosa make festoons of fairy tangle, but are disappointed to find no place to sit or rest, as the ground is alternately sandy or muddy from the irrigation which is necessary, as no rain worth mentioning falls and the vegetation is entirely dependent on the sluicing of the canals which intersect the land everywhere.

Ever wonder where you'd end up if you took your dog for a walk and never once pulled back on the leash?
ROBERT BRAULT

From the green depths of the garden comes the haunting, familiar sound of an Arab flute. We discover the player reclining in the shade of a mimosa tree, a boy of perhaps sixteen years with an intelligent face and dark, sombre eyes, which gaze at us with a strange unmeaning stare. He is very poor, judging from his one faded blue cotton garment, and we offer him backsheesh which to our amazement, he ignores. We discover that he is blind … the light of the golden day, the splendour of the starry nights are alike hidden from him; he lives in a land of shadows, his world is this plaintive, desolate music.

The date palm is largely cultivated here, forests of them stretching away as far as the eye can reach, a sight to gladden the Arab heart. Of all the gifts of nature in Egypt, the palm tree must surely rank first. Its trunk supplies the people with beams in a country where wood is practically non-existent.

☆ ☆ ☆

Though the carpet at our feet has failed us, the heavens above amply make up for it, as the sunset is gorgeous. Masses of pink, fleecy clouds trail along the blue ether and the slender new moon gleams occasionally through the rose mist. As we watch, it all changes to deep orange, then slowly becomes mauve as the sun sinks below the horizon and the evening star shines bright with a radiance that lights our earth. It is said that the star-light of Egypt is brighter than the moonlight of the North.

Wayfarers in the Libyan Desert (Arthur Humphreys, London, 1912)

A joyous spring day in Richmond Park, 1893
C.J. CORNISH

Richmond Park stretches out above the River Thames near London. As the author walked through the park on a spring day, he disturbed some of the creatures of the park.

The very dry and hot spring and early summer of 1893 were exceptionally favourable to all the birds and beasts which rear their young in the park. The last day of April was more like a hot June day, with all the freshness of young spring in the leaves of

Just living is not enough ... one must have sunshine, freedom, and a little flower.
HANS CHRISTIAN ANDERSEN

the trees; and the newly-arrived birds, as well as those which had spent the winter in the park, were revelling in the warmth. It was the most joyous spring day I ever remember. The trees seem to have all rushed into leaf together. The birds were almost beside themselves with happiness, which they showed each other after a fashion. All the spring warblers, resting after their journey over sea, were practising their song, wild ducks were flying in pairs over the lake – presumably mallards which were unoccupied with their broods – the lesser spotted woodpeckers, the cuckoos, redstarts, and wood pigeons were all uttering their spring notes. The deer were lying asleep, some of the stags stretched out with feet straight before them, and their chins resting on their knees, like a dog on a doorstep. Everything was happy, careless, and contented.

The fringe of the wood, in the centre of which the herons were silently brooding their young, was alive with the melody of birds and the movement of the smaller beasts with which, in addition to the red and fallow-deer, the park is now so abundantly stocked. Swarms of rabbits, old and young, were moving or sitting-up in the tussocks of dead grass among the birch-stems, wood-pigeons glided from tree to tree, so tame as to be almost indifferent to our intrusion, and the song of the wood-warbler, the chiff-chaff, the cuckoo, and the chaffinch, came from all parts of the grove. Within the outer circle of birch, the character of the wood changes. Tall young oaks and dark spruce-firs, with scattered clumps of rhododendron, take the place of the thick and feathery birch; and the song of the smaller birds was lost in the harsh and angry cries of the disturbed herons. A carrion-crow flapped from her nest on a dead oak, and flew with loud and warning croak through the centre of the wood; and a trespassing deer, springing from its form in which it was lying concealed like an Exmoor stag, crashed through the thick growth of rhododendrons, and added to the alarm of the colony.

Wild England of Today and the Wildlife in it (Seeley & Co, London, 1895)

I like girls who like the countryside, put on walking boots and can bend with the wind a bit. If you're going to live with me,

Woodstock, 1905
F.G. BRABANT

Many great country parks in Britain are open to the public where they may walk throughout the year for a small fee. Woodstock in Oxfordshire is one of the best known.

"The park is always open to pedestrians, but cycles are forbidden, and the grass must not be walked upon. The house and gardens can be seen on Tuesdays and Fridays in summer from 12 to 3pm."

The entrance to the park is at the West end of the main street of the town, and through a heavy triumphal arch, which the Duchess had erected the year after the Duke's death, with a Latin inscription outside and a translation of it on the inside.

On entering the town gate, the visitor has at once before him the lake, and the splendid bridge across it. When first constructed the bridge only spanned the narrow waters of the little Glyme, a contrast which provoked several epigrams. The authorship of the following is uncertain:-

> The minnows, as through this vast arch they pass,
> Cry "How like whales we look, thanks to your Grace."

Capability Brown, the celebrated landscape gardener, by damming up the Glyme, enriched the park with the present beautiful lake …

Most visitors will first walk round by the front of the palace to the bridge. Then crossing it, we have facing us, at some distance to the North, the Monument set up by the Duchess to the Duke. It is 134 feet high and contains a statue of the Duke at the top, and an account of his virtues and achievements on the pedestal.

Recrossing the bridge we have the front of Blenheim Palace immediately before us. As to its architectural merits, opinions will probably always differ …

Oxfordshire (Methuen, London, 1906)

you need to be able to embrace the countryside and wet dogs.
JAY KAY

Through the Cedars of Lebanon, 1847
HARRIET MARTINEAU

Having travelled from Egypt to Sinai, Harriet Martineau's group travelled on through Palestine to Lebanon and to the Cedars ...

These trees have now spread, from being a mere clump, to a wood of considerable extent. They stand on undulating ground – on a nook of hill and dale which is exceedingly pretty – its grassy and mossy surface shaded by the enormous old trees, and sprinkled all over with their seedlings. The priest who lives on the spot pointed out to us three trees which are declared to belong to the most ancient generations, and which devotees would fain make out to have been growing in Solomon's time.

There are nine more which look equally old; that is as old as possible. Of these nine, one measured 38 feet 11 inches round the trunk, and one of the three oldest measured 30 feet. It is under this last that Mass is performed once a year; and its trunk is carved all over with names. The priest told us that he had lived there, beside the little chapel, for twelve years, and that no accident had befallen any of the old trees in his time. The Christians call the trees 'Saints'; and when we asked how the Mohammedans regard them – knowing that they come hither in pilgrimage – we were told that they call them 'god-trees'. Their spread over the slopes is beautiful; and far down the declivities, their roots come out so woody and thick as to look like prostrate trunks. One of the second generation, the nine, is so strangely cut that we inquired the reason, and found that an Abyssinian monk lived in it for many years, in all weathers; till, at last, a rude hut of stones was built for him, which is still standing. The priest brought us wine, and gave us information very civilly. I would fain have stayed a day – or a week, if we could – for it is a charming spot; but it was thought necessary to proceed to Eden – nearly three hours further, on a rough and hilly road.*

* It was the custom for travellers to take cones and seeds from the Cedars home and grow them in their own gardens or estates. Wherever you see a Cedar of Lebanon growing today in Europe you can be almost certain that a distant owner of the estate travelled to the East. *Eastern Life* (Edward Moxon, London, 1848)

I find it a lot healthier for me to be someplace where I can go outside in my bare feet.
JAMES TAYLOR

Colour in the Duke of Lante's garden, 1909
SIR GEORGE SITWELL

Osbert Sitwell accompanied his eccentric father to Italy and, with him, walked in the garden of the Duke of Lante, near Viterbo. He quoted from his father's book, 'On the Making of Gardens'.

The Duke of Lante's garden is of another character, a place not of grandeur or tragedy but of enchanting loveliness, a paradise of gleaming water, gay flowers and golden light. The long, straight dusty road from Viterbo leads at length to a bridge across a deep ravine to a gap in the town walls of Bagnaia, 'twixt Gothic castle and Baroque church, then turning at a right angle to the piazza one sees in front of the great Renaissance gateway which opens into the garden. But it is better, if permission may be obtained, to enter the park, and striking upwards by green lawns and ilex groves to follow from its source the tiny streamlet upon which pool, cascade, and water-temple are threaded like pearls upon a string. Dropping from a ferny grotto between two pillared loggias, this rivulet rises again in an elaborate fountain surrounded by mossy benches set in the alcoves of a low box hedge. Four great plane-trees lift a canopy against the sun, and tall stone columns rising from a balustraded wall warn off the intruding woodland. Thence, running under ground, it emerges unexpectedly in the centre of a broad flight of steps between the claws of a giant crab – and races down a long scalloped trough and writhes like a huge snake over the carved shells which bar its passage.

Much there is of mystery in the garden, of subtle magic, of strange, elusive charm which must be felt but cannot be wholly understood. Much, no doubt, depends upon the setting, upon the ancient ilexes and wild mountain flank, the mighty hedge of green at the further end with its great pillared gateway and the dark walls and orange-lichened roofs of the houses and tower irregularly grouped behind it; upon the quiet background, the opal hues of green, violet and grey in the softly modelled plain, and shadowy outlines of the distant hills. But the soul of the garden is in the blue pools which, by some strange wizardry of the artist, to stair and terrace and window throw back the undimmed azure of the Italian sky.

On the Making of Gardens (John Murray, London, 1909)

Walking with royalty, May, 1662
WILLIAM SCHELLINKS

We went for a walk in St James Park, and from there into the King's Chapel, where there was glorious music; the King and the Duke of York came to attend the service, with their great garter jewels about their neck, and his Majesty dressed in purple. Coming from the chapel we went with Mr Uijenborgh again into St James's Park and saw there the new garden of the Duke of York, which is large and long, next to the Pall-Mall court. The Duke of York came to walk through the park, with the Garter on his left leg. We left St James' Park by the back exit and walked to Hyde Park, where every year on the first of May all the nobility from the court, town and country present themselves in their best finery, on horseback but mainly in carriages, so that they can see here the most beautiful ladies' dresses, horses, carriages, pages, liveries, etc, which can be seen anywhere in London, everybody trying to outdo the other in their dress in which they appear in public.

The Journal of William Schellinks' Travels in England, 1661-1663
(Royal Historical Society, London, 1993)

Like walking in a garden, 1879
ISABELLA BIRD

Miss Bird's letter to her sister from Malaya describes how she saw 176 varieties of trees and shrubs, 53 trailers, 17 parasites, and 28 ferns close by the track. Then she began to walk...

Wonderful as is the *Drosera Rotemdifolia* I think that the sensitive plant is more so. Touch the leaves which are tripartite ever so lightly and as quick as lightening they fold up. Touch the centre too ever so lightly and stalk and leaves fall smitten. Touch the branch

The less you carry the more you will see, the less you spend the more you will experience.
STEPHEN GRAHAM, *THE GENTLE ART OF TRAMPING*

and every leaf closes and every stalk falls with a great energy and as rapidly as the twinkling of an eye. Walk over it and you seem to have blasted the earth with a fiery tread, for every trailing plant falls and the leaves closing show their brown backs, and in a second are burned and withered. One could experiment on it all day.

After walking nearly 4 miles about the most glorious sight I have ever seen since leaving home appeared. A turn brought us upon a small lake behind which the mountains rose with a wall enclosing the house and coconut groves of the dispossessed Mentri of Larut on the slope beyond the lake. That was an unimaginable sight. Though a lake, no water was visible. From the water rose thousands and thousands of the leaves of the lotus peltate with wavy edges 18 inches in diameter, quite round, cool looking under the torrid sun, intense green but with a blue bloom like that on a plum. Above them rose thousands of lotus flowers buds and seed vessels, each one a thing of perfect beauty. The immense flowers varied from a deep rose crimson to a pink pale like that of a blush rose, some were just opening, others open, others wide open showing the crowded golden stamens and the golden disk in the centre. It was a most beautiful sight ....

Letters to Henrietta (The Leisure Hour, London, 1879)

The garden at Versailles, 1766
TOBIAS SMOLLETT

Smollett writes of his travels to his friends back in London – first reporting on his health...

With respect to my health about which you so kindly enquire, I have nothing new to communicate. I had reason to think that my bathing in the sea at Boulogne produced a good effect, in strengthening my relaxed fibres. You know how subject I was to colds in England; that I could not stir abroad after sun-set, nor expose myself to the smallest damp, nor walk till the least moisture appeared on my skin, without being laid out for ten days or a fortnight. At Paris, however, I went out every day, with my hat under my arm, though the weather was wet and cold: I walked in the garden at Versailles even after dark, with my head uncovered, on a cold evening, when the ground was far from being dry; nay, at Marli, I sauntered above a mile through damp alleys, and wet grass; and from none of these risques did I feel the least inconvenience.

Travels through France and Italy (R. Baldwin, London, 1766)

A garden in Ireland, 1950
ANNABEL DAVIS-GOFF

One of my favourite parts of a visit to a country house is the walled garden where one wanders through flowers, grass, fruit trees and even vegetables… like the garden described here.

Like Glenville, Ballinacourty had a wonderful walled garden. On entering through the latched wooden door, one found oneself in my grandmother's flower garden. It consisted of some semi-formal flower beds, in the centre of which lay a small lawn, slightly sunken and with a sprinkling of daisies and a slatted wooden garden bench. A well-placed apple tree or two helped separate this little garden from the larger one and made it a separate entity.

The garden was not completely symmetrical since at one time there had been a house or possibly a barn attached to it. The opening to this ruin remained, as did the outer walls of the building, and the area was used as a subsidiary vegetable garden.

The memories of the small garden with the lawn in the centre and of the second flower section, a herbaceous border facing a strip of lawn which led up to a large black fig tree in the corner, are warm and golden with a sense of well-being and sunshine. It was not only the delphiniums, dahlias, daisies and lupins which created this glow; it was physically warmer in the garden. The brick held the heat of the summer sun and the walls were high enough to keep out the wind and the sound of the wind. This garden was the quietest place in Ballinacourty.

Walled Gardens: Scenes from an Anglo-Irish Childhood (Knopf, New York, 1989)

A rainy day is the perfect time for a walk in the woods.
RACHEL CARSON

Through marble passages, 1851
FLORENCE NIGHTINGALE

On her return north, Florence Nightingale was taken to see the baths in Alexandria.

After a longish walk we came to a gateway, and through an avenue of date-palms, bananas, and petunias, trellised overhead, to a long, low building with Pompeian baths, in red and green and blue squares, and with low archways (against the heat), leading from one to the other. Egyptians sitting about at their dinner of fruits. They gave us a tangle of palm-tendrils to wash ourselves with, with a lump of beautiful Egyptian soap in the middle of the nest; all European appliances are vile compared to those palm-tendrils.

We came into an enormous square hall lined with marble, then through the marble passages into another octagonal vaulted court, lined, floor and roof, with marble, except where the roof was pierced with holes to let in spots and trails of brilliant sunlight. At the four corners were smaller halls, of immense height, with marble basins in each, the floors slippery with water, – the whole like an Arabian night.

I thought we were in the Chatsworth conservatory and should come out into the chill air, from all that radiant vegetation, and find it was a dream. But we did not.

☆ ☆ ☆

Then we went to church, – a little, quiet, solemn, English church, – and afterwards, Mr Winden, the clergyman, took us to the garden of the Armenians. Those Armenians always have something so poetic and mysterious about them. Fancy a church in the middle of alleys and tangles of palms, loaded with bunches of golden fruit, stretching every way into the forest, so that you lose the enclosure; daturas, bignonias, oleanders, cactuses, and bananas making the underwood; a great well in the midst, upon the edge of which sat the most beautiful group of Egyptian and Smyrniot women, and the radiant sunset behind.

On Mysticism and Eastern Religions, Volume 4 (1851)

Man's heart away from nature becomes hard.
STANDING BEAR

Measured for walking, 1870
AMELIA EDWARDS

Amelia Edwards' life – writing, working on the discipline of Egyptology, helping her friend – gave little time for recreation or exercise – unless she organised it….

I have no special working hours, because I work simply all day, all the morning, all the afternoon, all the evening – from the time I get up from the time I go to bed – saving and excepting only such times as I am at meals or taking exercise. At the Larches I have a straight path under the larch trees reaching from the entrance gate to the end of the lawn, which I have had measured. A register dial fixed on the greenhouse at the lower end of the lawn tells off 22 turns (I moving the index hand each time I reach the bottom).

The 22 make one mile. Winter and summer, rain, snow or sunshine, I walk half a mile before breakfast and ditto after breakfast, before beginning work. When tired of the desk, I rush out and do one quarter of a mile at various intervals during the day. In the afternoon, if my invalid is well enough, I go out with her for a couple of hours' drive, in the course of which we alight and walk a little. Besides this, I get another mile on the measured path before, or after, dinner – sometimes in the dark. I always make sure of two miles a day exercise , but generally get more.

Sometimes when Mrs Braysher is not well enough to go out, or the weather is not fit for her, I sometimes walk only in our own little domain, for weeks and weeks together, without once going outside the gates. My friends marvel how I can stand it; but the absolution from hat or bonnet is delightful, and I am quite happy.

Untrodden Peaks and Unfrequented Valleys (Longman's, Green & Co, London, 1873)

The place where you lose the trail is not necessarily the place where it ends.
TOM BROWN

The Almeda, and Santiago di Compostela, 2007
GUY ARNOLD

I went for a walk in the Almeda on a moonlight night; this is a beautiful formal park, one of whose ends overlooks the surrounding hills from a high point of the city. The park was virtually free of pilgrims almost all of whom remained hustling and bustling in the centre of the city although I did come across a young pilgrim couple who were so much in love that St James and all his works were for the first time being forgotten. They were sitting astride a bench facing one another as they ate their sandwiches, munching their way towards one another's lips, their packs and staves on the ground beside them, their eyes fixed forever on the future that only love can supply.

I returned to the cathedral in the afternoon to find it practically deserted so that I was able to admire its great arches and the extraordinary machinery on high which is used to swing the giant censers. Then I wandered the narrow streets, many of them oddly deserted once away from the magnetic attractions of the great plaza before the cathedral. I had not even considered trying to stay in Santiago and set off by bus to Vigo.

In the Footsteps of George Borrow: A journey through Spain and Portugal
(Signal Books, Oxford, 2007)

Near Jaffa, 1884
ANNIE C. MACLEOD

The path wound between rows of cacti or prickly pear, varying from three or four to fifteen feet in height; and one could not help pausing to look at their great soft fibrous stems fringed with 'leaves' resembling thick green cakes or 'bannocks' stuck with needles, and forming a defence through which the breeze can pass in full volume, but quite impervious to man or beast.

The gardens of fruit-bearing trees are the glory of Jaffa. There are endless groves of oranges and lemons, apricots, pomegranates, figs, and olives, with mulberry or acacia trees, the stately

When I walk with you I feel as if I had
a flower in my buttonhole.
WILLIAM MAKEPEACE THACKERAY

palm towering above them all. I was informed there were about three hundred and fifty gardens around this old town, the smallest being three or four acres in extent, the largest ten or twelve.

Of these gardens two hundred and fifty have one well, and about a hundred two wells each. Each well employs about three animals, who work day and night six months of the year, and draw each about one thousand cubic feet of water in the twenty four hours.

Half Hours in the Holy Land (The Half Hour Library, London, 1884)

The garden at Ashridge, 1933
CONSTANCE SITWELL

In her youth, she had visited the garden at Ashridge with a cousin and their German governess.

It was autumn when we were there, and at night, when the vast house lay so silent, surrounded by its famous beeches, its wet woods and the slopes and valleys of its beautiful park, we could hear in the damp hushed air the stags belling from far and near. On the short October afternoons we walked about the park with the governess; the moist, glistening beech-leaves were being swept into lines and heaps to be burnt; the woodmen on the estate used to wear scarlet jerseys then; the drifting smoke from the bonfires made the blue distance bluer. The smell of burning leaves always brings back those lovely curves of the ground with the fallow deer roving here and there, the patches of bracken, fading fern, the fading grass and shining tops of the beeches, brilliant as copper in the last rays of the sun as they struck across the valley.

But in the mornings, when we had finished our lessons, it was to the garden that we went; I don't remember ever reaching the end of it – it stretched so far; the 'pleasure grounds', as they were called, and walks, and thickets, and grottos; the round enclosed rose-garden, the monk's garden, where Elizabethan cloisters had been in the past, the Italian garden, with its great stone vases and formal beds; the ponds surrounded by square yew hedges; the lavender garden with its sundial and its herbs. It all seemed a little overwhelming to me after our house in the

I can enjoy society in a room; but out of doors, nature is company enough for me.
WILLIAM HAZLITT

middle of a village, where we had our friends so near at hand; I thought of its companionableness with longing sometimes, especially at night, when we went to bed, having said 'Good night' to the elders, robed in dignity and black crepe, and left them reading in what seemed to us a rather dreary silence in the library, lit only by its pools of light near their chairs, while the rest of the room remained dark in shadow.

We used to look out of the windows, when we got upstairs, and sniff the fresh autumnal air; sometimes we could hear the deer stirring near the house in the darkness; on windless nights the rustle of leaves falling, or chestnuts pattering down were the only sounds. But when there was a moon the deer could be seen moving about in the mist; if it lay thick on the ground we could not see their feet, but only their bodies and antlers emerging from the diaphanous haze …. *Petals and Places* (Jonathan Cape, London, 1935)

Lines written in Richmond Park, c. 1740
JAMES THOMSON

These lines were once written up on a board in Richmond Park, Surrey – still a wonderful place to walk, although 'graceful barks' may no longer be seen upon the river.

Richmond, ev'n now,
Thy living landscape spreads beneath my feet,
Calm as the sleep of infancy – the song
Of Nature's vocalists, the blossom'd shrubs,
The velvet verdure, and the o'er shadowing trees,
The cattle wading in the clear smooth stream;
And, mirrored on its surface, the deep glow
Of sunset, the white smoke and yonder church,
Half hid by the green foliage of the grove –
These are thy charms, fair Richmond, and through these
The river, wafting many a graceful bark,
Glides swiftly onward like a lovely dream,
Making the scene a Paradise.

The Seasons (P.W. Tomkins, London, 1797)

And forget not that the earth delights to feel your bare feet and the winds long to play with your hair.
KHALIL GIBRAN

8   WALKING BY WATER

Walking by water has special charms and special interests of many varieties. One may walk by a river, following it across nations – or by a stream with intimate glimpses of insights into nature. Along the tow path of a canal is a quiet place to walk with other walkers or in perfect solitude. One walks by the sea, with water splashing at one's feet. But there are other waters too: the hot waters which rise up in geysers like the famed Old Faithful in Yellowstone Park or other geysers in Iceland; there are the gentle waters of a country stream or the soft-flowing waters of a great river like the Nile or the Danube...

By the Thames, April 1662
WILLIAM SCHELLINKS

With a friend, Schellinks went on a tour by boat and on foot along the Thames from London, staying at pubs along the way.

From Richmond we walked along the River Thames. The tide does not come higher than (a few inches), so that it stagnates here, and the ships have to be towed up the river by the horses. There are many osier beds, where the boat men set their fish traps. We came through Petersham and across the river on the left saw a large deer park, which takes four hours to walk round.

At 8 o'clock we came to Kingston, a large market town, renowned for its antiquity. In olden times it was called the King's Town, or Kingston upon Thames. ... There is a wooden bridge over the river and one sees Hampton Court lying on the other side in Middlesex. In Kingston there is good fish to be had ...

The Journal of William Schellinks' Travels in England, 1661-1663
(Royal Historical Society, London, 1993)

Walking and watching, March 9, 1772
GILBERT WHITE

As a gentleman and myself were walking on the 4th of last
November, round the sea-banks at Newhaven, near the mouth of
the Lewes river, in pursuit of natural knowledge, we were surprised to see three house swallows gliding very swiftly by us.
That morning was rather chilly, with the wind at north-west; but
the tenor of the weather, for some time before, had been delicate,
and the noons remarkably warm. From this incident, and from
repeated accounts which I meet with, I am more and more
induced to believe that many of the swallow kind do not depart
from this island; but lay themselves up in holes and caverns; and
do, insect-like and bat-like, come forth at mild times, and then
retire again to their *latebrae*.

Nor make I the least doubt but that, if I lived at Newhaven,
Seaford, Brighthelmstone (Brighton), or any of those towns near
the chalk cliffs of the Sussex coast, by proper observations, I
should see swallows stirring at periods of the winter, when the
noons were soft and inviting, and the sun warm and invigorat-
ing. And I am the more of this opinion from what I have
remarked during some of our late springs, and though some
swallows did make their appearance about the usual time, viz.
the 13th or 14th of April, yet, meeting with a harsh reception, and
blustering, cold, north-east winds, they immediately withdrew,
absconding for several days, till the weather gave them better
encouragement.

The Natural History of Selborne (T. Bensley for B. White and Son, London, 1789)

Undress, 1860
BAYARD TAYLOR

The main road here left the valley, which nearly became next to
impracticable. We took a footpath up the stream, through a wild
glen half filled with immense fragments that had tumbled from
the rocky walls on either side. The close heat was like that of an

**Above all do not lose your desire to walk... I have walked
myself into my best thoughts and know of no thought so
burdensome that one cannot walk away from it.** THE BUDDHA

WALKING BY WATER

oven, and, as the solitude was complete, I gradually loaded my guide with one article of dress after another, until my costume resembled that of a Highlander, except that the kilt was white. Finally, seeing some haymakers at a point where the glen made a sharp turn, I resumed my original character; and it was as well that I did so, for on turning the corner I found myself in the village of Tuchersfeld, and in view of a multitude of women who were bleaching linen.

☆ ☆ ☆

Taylor recovered his composure, rested a while and then set off again.

For an hour and a half we walked through a deep, winding glen, where there was barely a little room here and there for a hay or barley-field. On the right hand were the tall forests of fir and pine; on the left, abrupt stony hills, capped with huge irregular bastions of Jura limestone. Gradually the rocks appear on the right and push away the woods; the stream is squeezed between a double row of Cyclopedean walls, which assume the wildest and most fantastic shapes, and finally threaten to lock together and cut off the path. These wonderful walls are three and four feet in height – not only perpendicular, but actually overhanging in many places.

As I was shuffling along, quite exhausted, I caught a glimpse of two naked youngsters in a shaded eddy of the stream. I was strongly tempted to join them; so I stepped down to the bank, and called out, "Is the water cold?"

Whoop! Away they went, out of the water and under a thick bush, leaving only four legs visible. Presently these also disappeared, and had it not been for two shirts more brown than white, lying on the grass, I might have supposed that I had surprised a pair of Nixies.

At Home and Abroad: A Sketchbook of Life, Scenery and Men
(George P Putnam, New York) 1860

... there's music in water. Brooks babbling, fountains splashing. Weirs, waterfalls; tumbling, gushing.
JULIE ANDREWS

Through Brazil, 1932
PETER FLEMING

There was some talk of crossing to the other bank after dark and taking compass bearings on anything that looked like a camp fire, so that in tomorrow's reconnaissance we should have some clue to work on. I wanted to have a look at the lie of the land; so while Queiros was making a fire, I stripped and tied a pair of trousers round my head and waded across. The water came up to my neck; the river was deeper here than we had known it since we had left Sao Domingo.

As usual, the open country on the other side was less open than it looked. The scattered trees and the tall grass made a screen which the eye could not penetrate in any great depth. About 400 yards inland there was a thickish belt of low scrub, and on the edge of it stood a tree with a broad but curiously twisted trunk. This I climbed.

I stayed up it for half an hour, and in that half hour the world below me changed. A wind began to sing in the sparse leaves round my observation post. The sky darkened. Massed black cohorts of clouds assembled in the west and came up across the sky under streaming pennons. The wind rose until its voice was a scream; great weals appeared in the upstanding grass, and in the straining thickets the undersides of leaves showed pale and quivering with panic. My tree groaned and bent and trembled. The sky grew darker still.

Brazilian Adventure (Jonathan Cape, London, 1933)

Early morning near Baalbec in Syria, 1856
REVEREND W. M. THOMSON

I am too deeply interested in these scenes to waste the morning hours in sleep. My first visit was to the fountain, to bathe and drink. I shall not lose the memory of that hour, should I live a thousand years. Then I followed the brook, crossed over to the

It's Niagara Falls. It's one of the most beautiful natural wonders in the world. Who wouldn't want to walk across it?
NIK WALLENDA (TIGHTROPE WALKER)

western side, and strolled away, I know not how far, among those venerable oaks. Returning, I climbed to the top of the castle on the north-west corner of the city, and looked and looked into the wilderness of bushes and briers that hides the brawling river at its base. Descending to some mills, I forced my way through sharp thorns, to the south-west corner, and then followed up the wall to the gate and bridge over the ravine called Saary, which, I suppose, formed the southern fosse of the city. From the north-eastern corner I followed the ditch, which brought me back to the tent.

The Land and the Book (Harper & Bros, New York, 1859)

The Llangollen Canal, 1985
ROGER W. SQUIRES & GARETH LOVETT JONES

This is the canal – on an aqueduct – with which many of us are familiar from pictures and few from experience. It was constructed early in the 19th century as part of the network of canals in Shropshire. It was an ambitious project, and still impresses us all today.

Our walk embraces the best of the canal and starts at Chirk Aqueduct, which bridges the border between England and Wales. The aqueduct is a master-piece of design, with its ten masonry arches supporting and embracing a cast-iron trough which is carried high over the wide valley of the River Ceiriog. The structure, designed by Telford, was opened in 1801 and is 696 feet long.

☆ ☆ ☆

Almost as soon as the canal has crossed the aqueduct it enters Chirk tunnel, some 459 yards long, with a wide railed towpath throughout. The tunnel is straight but the towpath in the tunnel is very uneven in places and the railings are rusted, which makes it sensible to take a torch, though often the lights of passing boats can guide the way. On leaving the tunnel, the canal enters a long, deeply wooded cutting. A sloping pathway joins the towpath from the right near the tunnel mouth and offers access to Chirk

It's a perfectly human instinct to want to be near water.
STONE GOSSARD

Station and to the road leading to the impressive and ornate wrought-iron gates of Chirk Castle.

Canal Walks (Hutchinson, London, 1985)

Bibury, 1904
C.R. BRANCH

After a slow start Mr Branch reached his intended place to walk. Bibury is one of my family's favourite places, and we try to visit the village every year. The countryside, it seems from Mr Branch's description, has changed more than the village of Bibury itself – pastures are no longer 'ablaze with colour' in June…

I may say at once that we eventually reached Bibury, that the walk through the flowery fields and along the by-roads of the Coln Valley, past grey towers and slumberous hamlets, past herds of inquisitive calves and sleek kine that grouped themselves in pastures ablaze with colour, was a real enjoyment; that the refreshment that followed a walk long enough to make a seat acceptable was better than most country inns afford; and that Bibury fully came up to expectation. I could understand the enthusiasm of the angler, for the Coln is a noted trout stream; and I could sympathise yet more fully with the eulogies that had been pronounced on the place by friends of the camera and canvas hobbies. … the prettiest village in Gloucestershire, unsurpassed and unsurpassable in its own way combining stream and bridge, broad meadows and majestic elms, cottage gables without a single modern eyesore to mar the picture, and noble Elizabethan architecture in stately manorial homes that carry the mind back to the days of Shakespeare and the chase of the red deer over the wild Cotswold country … among the many fair spots in England that are outside the beaten track of the sight-seer, there are few with greater charm than this.

Cotswold and Vale: or Glimpses of Past and Present in Gloucestershire
(Norman, Sawyer & Co, Cheltenham, 1909)

WALKING BY WATER

The world is mud-luscious and puddle-wonderful.
e.e. CUMMINGS

Rambling ashore, 1867
HOWARD HOPLEY

When sailing up the Nile, travellers would often leave the boat to walk along the bank so that they could see more of Egyptian life.

"Bring round the felucca; let us get on to the bank." So Saïd springs off to the captain, the captain shouts 'Yalla', and the sailors crowd their dusky limbs into the little boat. A few vigorous strokes of the oar over the placid and shining water, to that eternal chorus of *omm sowar* or *haylee sa*, and we are landed among the palms. Saïd stays with us, also Selim and Halil, to carry guns or game, and the felucca is sent back.

So we wander forth amid millet patches and stubble fields; amid the copses of acanthus and ricin which line the little creeks, where lazy buffaloes flounder with their nostrils just above the tide, steeping their ungainly bodies for half the day, and spluttering and mooing indolently at you with soft inward satisfaction; amid fields of cotton and palm-sheltered villages; and even away into the desert, – always and everywhere, be it understood, keeping a sharp eye from afar upon the whereabouts of the lateen sail and the long red streamer (of their boat).

Under Egyptian Palms: Or, Three Bachelors' Journeyings on the Nile (1869)

By the Thames, 1938
CHIANG YEE

One side of Battersea Park runs entirely by the river, where a short, stone wall has been built up the bank. There are many good trees planted there and no cars are running. I went there one morning and enjoyed the walk very much. Leaning on the low wall, I could watch the graceful flying of the sea-gulls. They seemed content with their food and just swung around steadily in circles in the air. Against a background of misty grey colour, I could not see any other movement but that of these white-winged birds. Some of them tried hard to fly against the mild

I roamed the countryside searching for answers to things I did not understand.
LEONARDO DA VINCI

wind or they just stretched their wings and let the wind bear them higher as if they were doing so purposely. Then I looked down on the surface of the water which seemed to me to be swaying slowly in the same direction as the gulls above. I could not help saying, "Rhythm is everywhere. Oh, the rhythm of nature!" In this park I like the lake particularly, where one can row, but the sound of trains and the smoke coming from two tall factory chimneys make me feel that I am not in a park at all.

The other part of the Thames I want to talk about is from Kew Gardens to Hampton Court and even farther. After strolling about in Kew Gardens for some time there is a very good place to sit and rest, by the side of the river. It is interesting; the trees leave a free space, and while I sit there I can listen to the sounds of the ripples breaking on the water. In the distance, on the other side of the river, there is a factory-like building with a trade-mark 'lion' on its roof, which makes me even more aware of my surroundings by the contrast. Occasionally I can also hear the people walking along the tow-path, which gives a sort of rhythmic sound. I remember once I walked there too, as far as Richmond. It is very pleasant to walk that way and I cannot describe how joyful a time it was for me. I seemed to be walking along the waterside of a big stream in China, if I forgot to look at the buildings on both sides. I fancy that the scene would be lovely in any kind of weather and season, and the interest always different. I have also thought that if there a bright moon hanging in the sky with a very clear atmosphere, I would like to stay there the whole night, and there might be one or two white swans floating on the water to keep me company!

The Silent Traveller in London (Country Life, London, 1938; rpt Signal Books, 2001)

A shepherd and his flock, 1856
REVEREND W.M. THOMSON

We are favoured with another bright morning, which you have been improving, as I see, by an early ramble over the hills; but come down to the river. There is something going forward worth seeing.

WALKING BY WATER

We have to walk in a way that we only print peace and serenity on the Earth. Walk as if you are kissing the Earth with your feet. THICH NHAT HANH

Yon shepherd is about to lead his flock across; and – as our Lord says of the good shepherd – you observe that he goes before, and the sheep follow. Not all in the same manner, however. Some enter boldly, and come straight across. These are the loved ones of the flock, who keep hard by the footsteps of the shepherd, whether sauntering through green meadows by the still waters, feeding upon the mountains, or resting at noon beneath the shadow of great rocks. And now others enter, but in doubt and alarm. Far from their guide, they miss the ford, and are carried down the river, some more, some less; and yet, one by one, they all struggle over and make good their landing.

Notice those little lambs. They refused to enter, and must be driven into the stream by the shepherd's dog, mentioned by Job in his 'parable'. Poor things! How they leap, and plunge, and bleat in terror! That weak one yonder will be swept away, and perish in the sea. But no; the shepherd himself leaps into the stream, lifts it into his bosom, and bears it trembling to the shore. All safely over, how happy they appear! The lambs frisk and gambol about in high spirits, while the older ones gather round their faithful guide, and look up to him in subdued but expressive thankfulness.

Now, can you watch such a scene and not think of that Shepherd who leadeth Joseph like a flock; and of another river, which all his sheep must cross! He, too, goes before, and, as in the case of this flock, they who keep near Him fear no evil.

The Land and the Book (Harper & Bros, New York, 1859)

In Italy, 1949
OSBERT SITWELL

Osbert Sitwell and his man servant, Henry, were in the Italian Lakes area. He was invited out to lunch by a friend.

By the hour the steamer, painted like a swallow, reached Fusina the atmosphere had cleared and the Venetian sun now defined every object with an unequalled and sparkling precision. It illumined for us, as we stood waiting on the road – built in case of floods, a little higher than the level of the land – every object within view very distinctly: but it did not show the motor-car we had been told to expect. Henry, however, observed that it was "a grand day for a walk" and, since this was plainly the truth, we adopted his proposal, and soon started to accomplish on foot the four miles along the side of that famous canal, the Brent, to the villa. As I watched Henry walking, I recognised that this was just the sort of off-maritime landscape he needed, to be seen in his perfection. The skin of his face, now generally copper-coloured from the effects of wind and sun, glowed a lusty red, and he swung his arms as he went with the jolly swagger of a fat man out for a day's enjoyment, the gaiety of the animal-paragon, who being contented in himself, can, though no longer young, still take pleasure in scent, sound and the feel of the air. Clad in a favourite blue suit and wearing black boots, square-toed, which he had only obtained as a bargain after much hard argument, he had crowned his head with the formidable dome of the bowler hat we have several times noted, and which did invariable duty as a cap of ceremony or maintenance. If he had been alone, I judged, he would have now broken into one of the more familiar and unctuous hymn-tunes that he so loved, as a chant to creation. Isolated after this fashion, in a globe of crystal above the canal on one side, and on the other a flat land intersected by gleaming lines of water, there still emanated from him and remained about him something unmistakably nautical; nature seemed to supply an immutable background of threshing whales, and analogy of porpoises that none could fail to perceive. In the mind's eye sea-gulls bumped and squealed in arcs round his head, their her-rings, their scales twinkling with light, weighed down the nets. … So we proceeded on our way, while the driver and our host's motor-car searched everywhere for us, since in Italy no one could be found to believe that two persons would of their own accord set out to walk so great a distance, we must, it was presumed, have been lost or gone mad.

Laughter in the Next Room: Left Hand, Right Hand Vol IV, (Macmillan, London, 1949)

There's something about the rhythm of walking, how, after about an hour and a half, the mind and body can't help getting in sync. BJORK

Around Port Meadow, 2008
OXFORD PEDESTRIANS ASSOCIATION

Port Meadow lies between the canal that runs through Oxford north to south and a tributary of the Thames. In winter it is often a very watery area with only areas of higher ground peering above the waters. Walking guides like this – often created by volunteers – open up a gateway to places to walk in many local areas, providing an intimate picture of both the historic and the modern features of a landscape. And – perhaps best of all – guiding the walker to the rights of way …

Enter Port Meadow through pedestrian gate at car park entrance, and turn left. However, do not follow the ditch at the back of the houses, but take path across grass a few degrees to the right. This goes to a bridge over a major ditch. Named Shiplake Ditch, it forms the boundary between Port Meadow and Wolvercote Common, marked by an 1899 stone about 30 metres to the right.

Having crossed the bridge, bear left towards the residential area of Lower Wolvercote and aim for the right end of the prominent three storey flat-roofed blocks. On the way you pass, on your right, a block of wartime allotments, still very productive, and an old sturdy gatepost surviving from an earlier enclosure.

On arrival at the urban edge, look closely at the boundaries on the far side of the ditch. The fourth plank bridge gives access through an old iron gate to a narrow right-of-way footpath. Follow this path as it winds on a route between old horse stables. These are reminders of the use of Port Meadow for traditional grazing of horses.

The right of Burgesses of Oxford to the pasture of Port Meadow was mentioned in the Domesday Book (1086). The right has continued to the present day, having devolved to the Commoners of Wolvercote, giving powers to them to graze cattle and horses, but not sheep, over the whole present area of the Meadow. Attempts by Oxford City Council between 16th and 20th centuries to enclose the land for financial gain were foiled.

Oxford on Foot (Oxford Pedestrians Association, 2008)

WALKING BY WATER

If one morning I walked on top of the water across the Potomac River, the headline that afternoon would read: 'President Can't Swim.' LYNDON B. JOHNSON

The uplands of Hell, 1900
RUDYARD KIPLING

Then by companies … we walked chattering to the uplands of Hell. They call it the Norris Geyser Basin on Earth. It was as though the tide of desolation had gone out, but would presently return, across innumerable acres of dazzling white geyser formation. There were no terraces here, but all other horrors. Not ten yards from the road a blast of steam shot up roaring every few seconds, a mud volcano spat filth to Heaven, streams of hot water rumbled under foot, plunged through the dead pines in steaming cataracts and died on a waste of white where green-grey, black-yellow, and pink pools roared, shouted, bubbled, or hissed as their wicked fancies prompted. By the look of the eye the place should have been frozen over. By the feel of the feet it was warm. I ventured out among the pools, carefully following tracks, but one unwary foot began to sink, a squirt of water followed, and having no desire to descend quick into Tophet I returned to the shore where the mud and the sulphur and the nameless fat ooze-vegetation of Lethe lay. But the very road rang as though built over a gulf; and besides, how was I to tell when the raving blast of steam would find its vent insufficient and blow the whole affair into Nirvana? There was a potent stench of stale eggs everywhere, and crystals of sulphur crumbled under the foot, and the glare of the sun on the white stuff was blinding.

From Sea to Sea; Letters of Travel, Volume 2 (1920)

Through Swaledale, 1940
WARD, LOCK & COMPANY, LTD.

Following the Reeth road westward from Richmond, we immediately have a foretaste of the beauties of Swaledale. Well-wooded hills rise steeply on either hem – trees cling even to the most precipitous rocks – and from the road there are glimpses of the river as it alternately brawls over its rocky bid or reflects the overhanging foliage in its mirror-like surface. In a few miles the hills

I stroll along serenely, with my eyes, my shoes, my rage, forgetting everything.
PABLO NERUDA

fall back and instead of trees we look up to heathery slopes falling to fields of that vivid green peculiar to the Dales.

On by Marske, Ellerton and Marrick Priory the Dale gradually opens out. So by the bridge over the Swale at Grinton and another at the entrance to the village we come to Reeth. The village is set around a large scree at the foot of Arkengarthdale and with views of the Dale up which we have come from Richmond, and around the hills – no longer the closely wooded cliffs by which we have passed, but bare slopes and shelves which are themselves an incitement to walkers; it is possible, too, to make a way up the riverside to Muker and Keld. Rising out of Reeth there is a grand view ahead of the Dale as it narrows along by Gunnerside, with the massive Great Shunner Fell beyond. Between Healaugh and Feetham on the left is the beginning of a fine walk over to Aysgarth and Bainbridge, in Wensleydale. Feetham overlooks the valley at a point where a road comes over from Arkengarthdale and Barnard Castle. Two miles farther is Gunnerside, a stone-built village at the foot of a narrow gorge up which there is a fine view to Keld, bearing left near the source of the stream then southward…

Ward Lock Red Guide: The Yorkshire Dales (Ward, Lock & Co, London, 1965)

Beside the Nile, 1856
WILLIAM C. PRIME

Travellers in Egypt would hire a boat in Cairo, sail south down the Nile and then sail back north with the stream.

As we approached Mansheeb I had walked along the shore ahead of the boat, and on reaching the village met Suleiman Aga, the local governor, taking a walk with his old uncle on the bank. He was apparently delighted at seeing the face of a stranger, for he said he lead a life of imprisonment in his village; and was glad of any relief to its monotony. He walked up the bank with me, and when the boat came to the land near the upper end of the village, he came on board and spent an hour with us. While we were lying here, our friends, the American missionaries, who were

**Falling leaves
hide the path
so quietly.** JOHN BAILEY, *AUTUMN HAIKU*

WALKING BY WATER

lying near us, had a difficulty with their servant, who was an impertinent scoundrel, and whom it became necessary for them to discharge. The governor begged hard to be allowed to thrash him into respectability, but to this, of course, our friends would not consent.

☆ ☆ ☆

Arriving at Luxor, Mr Prime was again off the boat, walking …

I left the Phantom and walked around the village, my foot-steps dogged by twenty donkey-boys, and as many donkeys, each of the former hoping that I would grow tired and patronize one of them. At every corner and turn a Coptic (Christian) scoundrel would produce a lot of antiques for sale, and I amused myself by asking prices.

The captain of Mr Prime's boat was eager to press on with the wind behind them.

But I could not go without one view over the plain, and at break of day I went up the hill to the foot of the propylon towers of the temple, and looked up to their summit. There must be a way to climb them, and while I was looking for it a bright Arab boy made his appearance and offered to show me. I followed him readily, and he led me through the propylon to the narrow alley already spoken of, and around the corner into a low door in the mud wall. This opened into a yard or court, full of sheep and *doura*, or corn-stalks, and passing through another like it, I climbed a mud wall and walked along this to the corner of the tower, which was somewhat broken. Climbing this some twenty feet and going around the end, I discovered an opening into the body of the tower, where, crawling in, I found a stairway, encumbered with huge masses of fallen stone, and up this I ascended, with no little difficulty, to the top of the tower. Here I sat and watched the coming of the sun. The Libyan hills (on the west of the Nile) were first lit, and the golden line of light came slowly down their rugged sides – down, down, until it reached the tombs that open to the east, and the Memnonium and Medeneet Habou, and then it touched the lips of Memnon and his old companion.* I saw the red flash on the giant head, and I bent my

WALKING BY WATER

I can't tell you how oppressive it is never to be able to go outdoors.
ANNE FRANK, *THE DIARY OF A YOUNG GIRL*

head forward to hear the sound of the salutation; but there was no sound – Memnon is vocal only in tradition.

* The great stone figures on the west bank of the Nile.

Boat Life in Egypt and Nubia (Harper & Bros, New York, 1857)

Mountains and sea, 2007
GUY ARNOLD

The last stretch of the coast that I walked was deep in Spanish holiday country. The ridge of the Mir del Fito mountains rose sharply from the coast to a height of twelve hundred metres to provide a perfect backdrop as I approached Ribadesella: sometimes I was in sight of the sea, at others it disappeared behind sand dunes or small hills. Once as I passed through a village, I heard a roaring noise somewhat like a train, a sound that was both familiar and strange at the same time, and only when I came in sight of the sea again did I realise its source as I saw the waves breaking on a great stretch of golden beach below me. It was a beautiful coast. At one point the road rose quite sharply into the hills and then I might catch a glimpse of the blue-green sea, beyond a spur, stretching to the horizon, or turn a corner to look down upon a little cove or bay of sparkling yellow sand, while at other times there was no hint that the sea was just over the nearby hills. Everything was green in the golden sunlight.

I took a mid-morning break outside a tiny shop on a hillside and watched a sleepy village come to life as the good people made their way to church, for it was a Sunday. The church was set back on a knoll overlooking the village below and the bell tolled from a white tower thrown into sharp relief by the green hills that rose beyond it. The people stood in groups, talking, greeting friends, and gradually disappearing into the church and then, at the last moment when the bell had ceased its call to the little community, some children came hurrying up the path when everyone else had disappeared inside.

In the Footsteps of George Borrow: A journey through Spain and Portugal
(Signal Books, Oxford, 2007)

There is scarcely any writer who has not celebrated the happiness of rural privacy, and delighted himself and his reader

By the sea shore, 1933
H.V. Morton

I took a narrow path over the dunes and came out on the sea shore. One of the most astonishing sights I have ever seen was spread out for miles on the edge of the Mediterranean.

Hundreds of camels were being given their annual bath. On the sand dunes at the back sat the crowds of women and children who had trekked down from every village in the district; the men and boys were engaged in the serious process of washing the camels. There was not, of course, one bathing costume among the camel washers, and they looked magnificent as their wet brown bodies caught the sun.

Groups of five or six pulled, prodded and pushed their camels into the breaking waves. Some camels resisted. Some started to kick. Some even broke loose and stampeded back to the women, pursued by wild and angry boys.

On the other hand many of the animals, once they had been persuaded to sit down in the sea, appeared to enjoy themselves. They refused to move! It was as difficult to get them out as it had been to get them in. They sat at the very edge of the sea, with their absurd supercilious heads lifted high above the advancing waves.

In the Steps of the Master (Rich & Cowan, London, 1934)

Along the canal, 1944
Chiang Yee

The climate of Oxford is not very different from the rest of England. Yet the heavy morning mist over the canal on summer mornings seems to belong to Oxford alone. I have developed a liking for this weather. When I wake up early and see the sun beginning to gleam through the mist I like to walk along the canal-bank before breakfast. On one of these walks I reached Aristotle Lane without seeing a soul. I walked slowly northwards from the bridge, in a morning mist so dense that I could scarcely

with the melody of birds, the whisper of groves, and the murmur of rivulets. Samuel Johnson

see before me. On one bank of the canal are fields adjoining the railroad, and on the other nothing but back gardens. Always a few yards ahead of me the canal-banks seemed to end in some mysterious manner, yet as I walked they opened up again. In fine, clear air the canal-banks might have appeared to me in all their sordid detail, but in the misty morning everything was transformed. A profusion of flowers grew in the back gardens of the houses, and their different colours tinged the shroud of mist with blobs of yellow, green and red, as I have seen elsewhere only in London parks. As I walked along I would see one of the blobs grow deeper in colour and a rose would stand out clearly on its slender stem as I passed, like a charming girlish face peeping out between pale-coloured curtains, shy but with graceful dignity. It was at such moments that I realised more vividly than ever the cunning of our great masters who would paint only a few flowers, gracefully arranged, and give a masterpiece to the world. What more is needed?

The Silent Traveller in Oxford (Methuen, London 1944; rpt Signal Books, Oxford 2001)

By sea and land, Monday, 6th November, 1837
LADY JANE FRANKLIN

Newly arrived in Tasmania, one of the convict colonies of the time, Lady Franklin was learning much about the country. There were, at the time, paths but no proper roads.

It was a very showery day. About 10 we left Clark's in his boat and were landed on the bush-covered part of his swamp below, being part of the 640 acres lately purchased, and just where the side line is traced between Clark's and Captain Ross's division of it. Clark had already partially cleared by contract 25 acres of his own portion adjoining his old farm and has potatoes planted in it. I wished to tread upon and look at a fair specimen of his land and took with me a box to bring away some of the mould in. There is a tolerably good footpath thro' the bush swamp made by the splitters who have been at work here, and who threw down some branches and logs across the path to facilitate their own

Keep close to Nature's heart ... and break clear away, once in awhile, and climb a mountain or spend a week in the woods. Wash your spirit clean. JOHN MUIR

passage when loaded with heavy burdens and cut steps in the prostrate trunks of trees for the same purpose. We passed a rude half ruined hut which has been inhabited by three people and some fine trees. The ground rises beyond and after proceeding a little way, we stopped short at a prostrate swamp gum, which has been partly used for splitting, and round about which the soil being of an average good quality, not the very best, yet much farther removed from being the worst, – I filled one of the divisions of my box with it. ….

Returning to the boat we saw the schooner party, Sir John, the Bishop, Sophy, Miss Williamson and William Kerr advancing up the river in their boat. We greeted them on their arrival amidst a swarm of mosquitoes which infested the shore of the swamp, and as we pushed off saw them disappear one by one in the bush by the same inlet we had made use of. Mrs Gell remarked of them that they were all as it were strangers and birds of passage in these regions except the Bishop who was part of the Natural History of the Country, the same as the birds and the trees.

Some Private Correspondence, Tasmania, Vols xvii & xviii (ed. Geo Mackaness, 1837-45)

Settle towards Stackhouse, 1923
FREDERIC RILEY

This description of a walk bears all the marks of a walker who has passed this way on several occasions at different seasons of the year …

One of the most popular riverside rambles from Settle is to Stainforth Foss*, by way of the Ribble valley. This route demands no undue exertion in the way of climbing, and forms an enjoyable half-day excursion.

Upon arriving at the Ribble Bridge, a stile at the north-west end leads through the fields to Stackhouse Lane. On reaching the lane turn to the right for Stackhouse, which is approached beneath a canopy of trees and sylvan surroundings reminiscent of some Devonshire lane. For beauty of situation Stackhouse has few equals; its clustered, well-built houses set amid the trees, with the beech wood background and limestone scars above,

WALKING BY WATER

When you see someone putting on his Big Boots, you can be pretty sure that an Adventure is going to happen.
A.A. MILNE, *WINNIE-THE-POOH*

form an attractive picture. Although tree-felling of late years has robbed Stackhouse of many fine specimens it still remains the best wooded hamlet for miles around.

The road onward past Stackhouse leads to Knight Stainforth, and may be followed if the weather be too wet for field paths. For the latter and more picturesque route, pass down the old lane to the right leading to the Ribble, where a wooden bridge affords access to Langciffe. Do not cross the bridge, but turn to the left and pass over a step-stile near the weir.

Pleasant indeed is the journey onward, where the river flows by verdant banks, gay with primrose in spring, and many coloured flowers in summer. Few stretches of river attract a greater variety of bird life. The kingfisher is often seen here, and the heron, among other typical birds of the stream, frequents the neighbourhood. The belt of woodland passed on the left is the abode and haunt of many forms of wild life. The Paper Mill on the opposite bank of the river represents one of the oldest industries along the Ribble.

The path onward still follows the river, and passes beneath an avenue of trees before reaching the Foss. In wet weather this woodland path, where it runs by the side of the river, is inclined to be slippery, and it is then better to take the path on the left-hand side of the wall.

Stainforth Foss and its immediate surroundings form one of the most picturesque bits of scenery along the whole length of the Ribble. The stream from above flows through a well-wooded glade, passing beneath the graceful one-arch bridge, a short distance below which it falls over a succession of limestone ledges into a circular pool thirty feet deep. Stainforth Bridge is a now a possession of the National Trust. The wood to the left, north of the bridge, may be entered and one may follow the path, at the termination of which there once stood a small cotton mill, one of many others in the district. Part of the old mill race may still be traced.

* Foss or Fosse is a long, narrow ditch – which may be a moat or fortification.

The Settle District and North West Yorkshire Dales A Practical Guide Book for the Visitor and Tourist (Settle, 1923)

It seems very safe to me to be surrounded by green growing things and water.
BARBARA KINGSOLVER

WALKING IN TOWNS AND CITIES

9

Cities are so varied that walking through them can provide visual interest almost as varied as that to be seen when walking in the countryside. How different New York is to Venice or London to Paris! They also have varied over time – so the city in which a 19th-century traveller walked may be very different today. Perhaps only Venice remains almost unchanged …

The bazaars of Cairo, 1897
EUSTACE A. REYNOLDS-BALL

The Khan Khalil was built in 1292, by the famous Mameluke Sultan, El-Ashraf, the conqueror of Acre. It is on the site of the Tombs of the Caliphs. This is the chief emporium for carpets, rugs, and embroidered stuffs. … In one part of the khan is a place reserved for dealers in brass and copper goods.

Crossing the street Suk-en-Nahhassin, we come to the Suk-es-Saigh (gold and silversmiths' bazaar), a much frequented resort for tourists. The workmanship and quality of the trinkets has greatly deteriorated of late. In fact, old Cairo residents among the foreign colony declare that many of the jewels have a Palais Royal or Birmingham origin.

Continuing northwards and turning to the right, we reach the Gamaliyeh (camel-drivers') quarter. Here are the shops of the Red Sea traders. Very inferior goods are usually only available here, the chief commodities being incense, perfumes, spices, mother-of-pearl, and attar of roses. The latter is so much diluted that it is almost worthless, a small flask being sold for a franc or so, which would cost at least a pound if pure. The northern continuation of the street forms the coppersmiths' bazaar; and here also are booths for the sale of pipes, cigar-holders, amber, narghilehs, chibouques, and other articles for smokers. Retracing our steps to the starting-point, and crossing the Rue Neuve, – as absurdly named as New College in Oxford, for it is one of the oldest streets, – we reach the once flourishing Suk-es-Sudan, which, though mentioned in the guide-books, no longer exists, since the Soudan has been practically closed to traders. In this quarter are also the book-sellers' bazaar, of little interest, and the Suk-el-Attarin (spices, perfumes, etc), one of the most characteristic bazaars.

The City of the Caliphs (Estes & Laurait, Boston, 1897)

Third Girl, 1966
AGATHA CHRISTIE

Hercule Poirot walked along the main street of Long Basing. That is, if you can describe as a main street a street that is to all intents and purposes the only street, which was the case in Long Basing. It was one of those villages that exhibit a tendency to length without breadth. It had an impressive church with a tall tower and a yew tree of elderly dignity in its churchyard. It had its full quota of village shops disclosing much variety. It had two antique shops, one mostly consisting of stripped pine chimney pieces, the other disclosing a full house of piled up ancient maps, a good deal of porcelain, most of it chipped, some worm-eaten old oak chests, shelves of glass, some Victorian silver, all somewhat hampered in display by lack of space. There were two cafés, both rather nasty, there was a basket shop, quite delightful, with a variety of home-made wares, there was a post office-cum-greengrocer, there was a draper's which dealt largely in millinery and also a shoe department for children and a large miscellaneous selection of haberdashery of all kinds. There was a stationery and newspaper shop which also dealt in tobacco and sweets. There was a wool shop which was clearly the aristocrat of the place. Two white-haired severe women were in charge of shelves and shelves of knitting materials of every description. Also large

WALKING IN
TOWNS & CITIES

Walking is also an ambulation of mind.
GRETEL EHRLICH

quantities of dress-making patterns and knitting patterns and a counter for art needle-work. What had lately been the local grocer's had now blossomed into calling itself a 'supermarket' complete with stacks of wire baskets and packaged materials of every cereal and cleaning materials all in dazzling paper boxes.

And there was a small establishment with one small window with Lillah written across it in fancy letters, a fashion display of one French blouse, labelled 'latest chic' , and a heavy skirt and a purple striped jumper labelled 'separates'. These were displayed by being flung down as by a careless hand in the window.

All of this Poirot observed with a detached interest ... Poirot walked gently along digesting all that he saw.

Third Girl (The Crime Club Collins, London, 1966)

In Moscow, 1937
J.B. PRIESTLEY

After I had explored my immediate surroundings in Dubrovka and Orekhovo, I spent many free days in the capital, Moscow. Moscow was about sixty-five miles away from Orekhova and there were nine or ten trains a day in each direction. The fare was only one rouble 90 kopeks, or about 4½ pence. There was no special reduction for day or monthly return tickets.

☆ ☆ ☆

The probable explanation of why so many visitors come back from Moscow with such totally contradictory stories about conditions in Russia is that you can see there exactly what you decided to see before you went out there. You can see tall, splendid modern buildings, you can see tumble-down little wooden shacks. They are both there, cheek by jowl, and it is scarcely necessary to say which are Soviet and which are Tsarist. You can see in one street the latest fifteen-foot American motor snow-sweeper, and in the next street an old peasant woman patiently sweeping up the leaves with a brush with about three hairs left on it. These things are typical of the transition stage through which the Soviet

WALKING IN
TOWNS & CITIES

No city should be too large for a man to walk out of in a morning. CYRIL CONNOLLY

Union is passing, a transition often too abrupt for the Russian mind fully to adapt itself to ...

☆ ☆ ☆

Priestley, like many others before and after him, walked around the centre of Moscow.

In the centre of the city is the Kremlin, a great triangular "city within a city", surrounded by forbidding high walls, but across the river can be seen green lawns and the spires of countless chapels. Here live Stalin and most of the other members of the inner circle of commissars and high officials. It is the nerve-centre from which the vast Soviet Union is ruled with a grip more absolute than any Tsar has ever held. Could those walls but speak, what ardent controversies they could solve.

On the three half-mile walls of the Kremlin, one runs along the bank of the river Moscva , another is flanked by open spaces, museums, and Academies, and the third faces onto the famous Red Square and across that to the offices of the Central Committee and the Commissariat of Defence. At the lower end of Red Square stands the church of St Basil, one of the most amazing architectural oddities. This was built to the order of the Tsar, Ivan the Terrible. It looks as if a child had been let loose with a box of bricks; domes, spires, and buttresses grow out without symmetry or plan on every side.

Rain Upon Godshill, A Further Chapter of Autobiography (Heinemann, London, 1939)

To the sacred place – Eyoub, 1921
Pierre Loti

I took my son to Eyoub. Since his first visit to Turkey six years ago, it had been his dream to see the silent courtyards of the mosque of Eyoub, the most sacred place in Constantinople, the only one which was jealously forbidden to strangers. Until now, I had always refused to take my son there, because I was a little afraid.

I no longer want to walk on worn soles.
Friedrich Nietzsche

To give ourselves the air of people of the country, I judged it prudent to arrive at Eyoub via the great cemeteries and to approach the perimeter of the mosque from the side facing the Golden Horn.

Clothed in fezzes and our beads in our hands like good Turks, we opened the little gate which closes the sacred courts and found ourselves in the midst of a green night of tall cypresses and broad planes whose age no one knows. There, below the venerable stelae with their stone turbans, sleep the companions of Mehmed II in this vast enclosure of silence, whose walls are adorned with old ceramic work with blue flowers. Some pious old men were crouched in prayer, while the pigeons and the swans walked familiarly around them on the flagstones.

We pass quietly, without attracting attention, into this place whose peace is so profound as to be oppressive and arrive before the kiosk where the Saint Eyoub sleeps. We halt to admire the tomb though the bronze grill of one of the windows. The interior of this kiosk, which is situated slightly below the level of the court, is occupied almost entirely by the great catafalque covered with silk shot with gold and surmounted by an enormous turban.

All around the walls glitter in their covering of ancient faience, with designs in the most beautiful red, that ruby red whose secret has been lost for three centuries.

Shut in close to the catafalque, with his back to us, an ancient hoca, seated on his haunches, reads the Koran in a precious manuscript of parchment illuminated with gold. Perhaps we stay too long looking at these things, for the old hoca, as if he had scented infidels, turns sharply towards us and regards us with a mistrustful air which suddenly frightens us; we suddenly have the uncomfortable sensation of being intruders, profaning a sacred place. Nonetheless, it will not do to appear disturbed, which would immediately arouse alarm, and we depart without hurrying, telling our beads.

Istanbul (Casterman, Paris, 1992)

WALKING IN
TOWNS & CITIES

We live in a fast-paced society.
Walking slows us down. ROBERT SWEETGALL

Walking in Bath, 1890
KARL BAEDEKER

Bath, the chief place in Somerset, is a handsome town of fifty three thousand seven hundred and sixty one inhabitants, beautifully situated in the valley of Avon and on the slopes of the surrounding hills, and is perhaps unrivalled among provincial English towns for its combination of archaeological, historic, scenic, and social interest. It is a city of crescents and terraces, built in a very substantial manner of a fine grey lime stone, and rising tier above tier to a height of about six hundred feet. Among the most characteristic streets are the Royal, Lansdown, and Camden Crescents, the Circus, Pulteney Street, all of which recall similar streets in Edinburgh.

Bath is surrounded with "Downs", softly rounded hills, the tops of which afford charming views … A walk or drive over Lansdown as far as the third milestone and thence (for walkers only) across the racecourse to Prospect Stile will afford the visitor one of the finest views in the west of England. On the way we pass, after two miles, Lansdown Cemetery, with the tomb of Beckford of Fonthill and a tower built by him, the top of which commands an extensive view. This walk may be lengthened by returning through North Stoke (with an ancient church) and thence through Upton or Bilton to the railway.

Baedeker's *Great Britain* (Karl Baedeker, Leipzig, 1890)

By the Red Sea, 1909
ARTHUR E.P. WEIGALL

After breakfast next morning we walked along the beach to the stiff, mustard-coloured government buildings, which stand on a point of land projecting somewhat into the sea. A spick-and-span pier and quay, ornamented with three or four old French cannon and neat piles of cannon-balls, gave us the impression that we had been transported suddenly to a small English watering place; but passing into the building that impression was happily

I have the European urge to use my feet when a drive can be dispensed with.
VLADIMIR NABOKOV, *LOLITA*

removed at once. Through the sunny courtyard we went, and up the stair, saluted at intervals by the coastguardsmen, who had donned their best uniforms for the occasion, and at last we were ushered into the presence of our Maltese friend, now seated at state at his office table at the far end of a large airy room. The windows overlooked the glorious blue sea and the breath of an ordinary English summer drifted into the room bringing with it the sigh of the waves … When they left, there was the silence of sleep upon the place, and, returning to the almost deserted lanes between the houses outside, there was hardly a sound to disturb the silence of the morning. In the bazaar, a few people gathered around the two or three shops, at which business had now ceased. Soon we passed the open door of the schoolroom, where a dozen children chanted their Arabic ABC in a melancholy minor; and presently we came to the chief sight of Kossair – the old fortress built by the French at the end of the eighteenth century.

There are still three or four cannon inside it to tell of its past life, but now the rooms and courts are whitewashed and are used as camel stables by the coastguards.

Travels in the Upper Egyptian Desert (Thornton Butterworth, London, 1909)

Along Watling Street, 1971
J.H.B. PEEL

The sun and the song and the lanes and the fields were further away than I had reckoned, because Time itself had flown faster than I had reckoned, obliterating almost the whole of my slight acquaintance with suburban London … To be brief and honest, I found nothing of interest to report until I entered St Albans via a modern main road. The invisible Watling Street entered via London Gate and the massive Roman wall there, which is overlooked by the Verulam housing estate. I walked slowly along the length of that wall – more than a hundred yards of it – until a spacious green appeared, and beyond it the hill overlooking the Roman city of Verulamium, razed by Queen Boudicca, rebuilt by the Romans larger than before, encircling two hundred acres with a wall … Although it is no longer possible to follow Watling Street through St Albans, excavation has revealed that it passed north of Forum, close to St Michael's church, thence closed to the Roman theatre and into the more or less open country of Hertfordshire.

Along the Roman Roads of Britain (Cassell, London, 1971)

The sounds and smells of the streets of Cairo, 1920
RUDYARD KIPLING

Walking through a city one sees so very much more than one would ever see if passing in a car or even a horse-drawn vehicle.

… The city thrust more treasure upon me than I could carry away. It came out of dark alleyways on tawny camels loaded with pots; on pattering asses half buried under nets of cut clover; in the exquisitely modelled hands of little children scurrying home from the cookshop with the evening meal, chin pressed against the platter's edge and eyes round with responsibility above the pile; in the broken lights from jutting rooms overhead, where the women lie, chin between palms, looking out of windows not a foot from the floor; in every glimpse into every courtyard, where the men smoke by the tank; in the heaps of rubbish and rotten bricks that flanked newly painted houses, waiting to be built, some day, into houses once more; in the slap and slide of the heel-less red-and-yellow slippers all around, and, above all, in the mixed delicious smells of frying butter, Mohammadan bread, kebabs, leather, cooking-smoke, assafetida, peppers, and turmeric. Devils cannot abide the smell of burning turmeric, but the right-minded man loves it. It stands for evening that brings all home, in the dish, the one face, the dropped veil, and the big guttering pipe afterwards.

From Sea to Sea; Letters of Travel, Volume 2, (1920)

WALKING IN
TOWNS & CITIES

If you pick 'em up, O Lord, I'll put 'em down.
ANON *PRAYER OF THE TIRED WALKER*

Some problems, 2004
CHARLIE CONNELLY

I'd crossed the A140 without mishap and plunged into a network of suburban crescents full of timbered modern housing – that all seemed to lead me back to precisely where I'd started. I studied the map, failed to see where I'd gone wrong and headed in again. The fact that the streets and houses all looked the same, even down to the shrubbery in the front gardens and the silver cars in the driveways, didn't help and again I'd ended up right back where I'd started. Yet again I traced with my finger the route that irrefutably lead to the road to Diss, and walked back into the maze of streets before irrefutably arriving right back where I'd started. I tried twice more, the same result. Never mind, I thought, I'll wake up in the Norwich Travelodge in a minute and this will all have been a big, snuffling, sweaty anxiety dream … I trudged back to the main road and its relentless traffic. I looked south. Somewhere down there was Diss. I looked back towards the groundhog suburbia I'd just left, sighed, shifted the rucksack, took half a dozen reluctant steps and then saw it. On the other side of the road. About two hundred yards away. The bus stop.

I couldn't possibly. Could I? I consulted the map again … Surely I couldn't give in and take the bus, not on the first day …

Attention all Shipping: A Journey round the Shipping Forecast
(Little Brown, London, 2004)

WALKING IN
TOWNS & CITIES

A line is a dot that went for a walk.
PAUL KLEE

10

WALKING AT NIGHT

In the dark we walk more slowly, more carefully. If the ground is unfamiliar, we watch every step – more aware of the immediate space around us than in daylight. As Henry Thoreau recorded, at night, instead of the sun there is the moon, instead of butterflies, fire-flies – even the air smells different …

The end of the day, 1908
KENNETH GRAHAME

The sheep ran huddling together against the hurdles, blowing out thin nostrils and stamping with delicate fore-feet, their heads thrown back and a light stream rising from the crowded sheep-pen into the frosty air, as the two animals hasted by in high spirits, with much chatter and laughter.

They were returning across country after a long day's outing with Otter, hunting and exploring on the wide uplands where certain streams tributary to their own river had their first small beginnings; and the shades of the short winter day were closing in on them and they had still some distance to go. Plodding at random across the plough, they had heard the sheep and had made for them; and now, leading from the sheep-pen they found a beaten track that made walking a lighter business, and responded, moreover, to that small inquiring something which all animals carry inside them, saying unmistakably, "Yes, quite right; this leads home!"

"It looks as if we were coming to a village," said the Mole somewhat dubiously, slackening his pace, as the track, that had in time become a path and then had developed into a lane, now handed them over to the charge of a well-metalled road. The animals did not hold with villages, and their own highways, thickly frequented as they were, took an independent course, regardless of church, post office, or public house.

The Wind in the Willows (Methuen, London, 1908)

Lost, 1880
MARK TWAIN

Of course, not all walking is enjoyable – even in retrospect. Having set out early, Twain and his friend found themselves in trouble .....

The night shut down, dark and drizzly, and cold. About eight in the evening the fog lifted and showed us a well-worn path which led up a very steep rise to the left. We took it, and as soon as we had got far enough from the railway to render the finding it again an impossibility, the fog shut down on us once more. We were in a bleak unsheltered place now, and had to trudge right along in order to keep warm, though we rather expected to go over a precipice sooner or later. About nine o'clock we made an important discovery – that we were not on any path. We groped around a while on our hands and knees, but could not find it; so we sat down in the mud and the wet scant grass to wait. We were terrified into this by being suddenly confronted with a vast body which showed itself vaguely for an instant, and in the next instant was smothered in the fog again. It was really the hotel we were after, monstrously magnified by the fog, but we took it for the face of a precipice and decided not to claw up it.

A Tramp Abroad (American Publishing Co, 1880)

Moonlight, 1899
ELIZABETH VON ARNIM

June 16th. – Yesterday morning I got up at three o'clock and stole through the echoing passages and strange dark rooms, undid with trembling hands the bolts of the door to the verandah, and passed out into a wonderful, unknown world. I stood for a few minutes motionless on the steps, almost frightened by the awful purity of nature when all sin and ugliness is shut up and asleep, and there is nothing but the beauty left. It was quite light, yet a bright moon hung in the cloudless grey-blue sky; the flowers were all awake, saturating the air with scent; and a nightingale

Slowly, silently, now the moon
Walks the night in her silver shoon.
WALTER DE LA MARE

sat on a hornbeam quite close to me, in loud raptures at the coming of the sun. There in front of me was the sun-dial, there were the rose bushes, there was the bunch of pansies I had dropped the night before still lying on the path, but how strange and unfamiliar it all looked, and how holy – as though God must be working there in the cool of the day. I went down the path leading to the stream on the east side of the garden, brushing aside the rockets that were bending across it drowsy with dew, the larkspurs on either side of me rearing their spikes of heavenly blue against the steely blue of the sky, and the huge poppies like splashes of blood against the greys and blues and faint pearly whites of the innocent, new-born day. On the garden side of the stream there is a long row of silver birches, and on the other side a rye-field reaching across in powdery grey waves to the part of the sky where a solemn glow was already burning. I sat down on the twisted, half-fallen trunk of a birch and waited, my feet in the long grass and my slippers soaking in dew.

Through the trees I could see the house with its closed shutters and drawn blinds, the people in it all missing, as I have missed day after day, the beauty of life at that hour. Just behind me the border of rockets and larkspurs came to an end, and, turning my head to watch a stealthy cat, my face brushed against a wet truss of blossom and got its first morning washing. It was wonderfully quiet, and the nightingale on the hornbeam had everything to itself as I sat motionless watching that glow in the east burning redder; wonderfully quiet, and so wonderfully beautiful because one associates light with people, and voices and bustle, and hurryings to and fro, and the dreariness of working to feed our bodies, and feeding our bodies that we may be able to work to feed them again; but here was the world wide awake and yet only for me, all the fragrance breathed only by me, not a living soul hearing the nightingale but me, the sun in a few moments coming up to warm only me, and nowhere a single hard word being spoken, or a signal selfish thing being done, nowhere anything that could tarnish the blessed purity of the world as God has given it us.

The Solitary Summer (Macmillan & Co, London, 1899)

In the morning a man walks with his whole body; in the evening, only with his legs. RALPH WALDO EMERSON

Walking with the moon, 1938
CHIANG YEE

In London I can only enjoy looking at the moon some time very late at night. It is best after one o'clock in the morning and it is best of all in September and October, when the English call her harvest moon and hunting moon. I cannot walk very far from my lodgings late at night, because there is no late service train or bus. Once an American lady friend of mine told me that her compatriots wrote that "only rich people are allowed to live in London because they can go about late at night in their own cars." This is very true. I do not mind being poor and having no car but I do mind if the policeman comes to disturb my tranquil walk late at night. One night I was attending a dinner party in Chelsea and afterwards a friend of mine drove me home with him in his car. It was a very clear night and we were so late that the streets were completely empty. As soon as we reached Camden Town, I thanked my friend for having brought me so far and begged him to drop me there. Of course I did not tell him the reason why. At last he let me out so I could walk and look at the moon on my way home, as I have written a line in one of my poems "The bright moon escorting me home."

On both sides of the street it was quiet and there was nobody about. I did not know why I felt the moonlight was a stranger to those street lamps. And I felt her brilliance was stronger than theirs too – they were dwarfs by comparison. Once or twice I wondered if I was going to meet a policeman, because I had been told that they would ask me why I was walking so late and would take me to the police station. I did not mind their doing so if I could not find my way home – that would mean a shelter for me. Suddenly I saw a shadow coming out from a corner of the street in the distance. At first I thought it was coming towards me, but afterwards it disappeared. Then I came to Chalk Farm tube station. As I continued up Haverstock Hill Road, the moon shone on me even more brightly than before and I thought I was walking nearer to her step by step.

The Silent Traveller in London (Country Life, London, 1938; rpt Signal Books, 2001)

If you are seeking creative ideas, go out walking. Angels whisper to a man when he goes for a walk. RAYMOND INMON

Into an underground wilderness, 1932
H.V. MORTON

… one night, just before moonrise, we went down to the Zion Gate and took those dark, mysterious roads that lie beyond the walls of Jerusalem and lead steeply down into the Valley of Hinnom, which is Ge Hinnom or Gehenna – otherwise Hell. It was in this valley that the abominable rites of Bal were observed, and somewhere in it once stood the fires of Moloch in which children were sacrificed.

We went down into a stony wilderness bleached white by the thousands of grave-stones which rise on both slopes of the valley, marking the graves of Jews and Moslems who wish to be first on the Resurrection morning. A few lights on the hill marked the squalid little village of Siloam. Somewhere in the darkness to our right was the Field of Blood, which the Chief Priests bought with the silver of Judas.

We had to pick our way carefully, flashing electric torches on the stony track. Behind us came an Arab carrying lanterns and thigh boots.

While we stumbled downward in single file, sometimes straying from the path and tripping over stones, I thought how astonishing it is that, while so much of old Jerusalem has perished, this tunnel of Hezekiah, one of its earliest relics, should exist today almost as it was seven hundred years before Christ.

☆ ☆ ☆

We came down to the Pool of Siloam, where we put on our waders by a light of a torch held by the Arab. The tunnel was a black hole in the side of the hill, from which water about two feet in depth was flowing. There was a weird echo in it, as if people were whispering in the darkness.

"There's nobody there," said my friend. "No Arab would go through the tunnel at night. We are hearing echoes from a mosque on the hill."

As we waded into the tunnel our electric torches lit up the flow of brownish water and the clammy walls. The cutting was

I cannot walk through the suburbs in the solitude of the night without thinking that the night pleases us because it suppresses idle details, just as memory does. JORGE LUIS BORGES

perhaps fourteen feet high and only two feet wide, but the height was never the same for very long. The marks made by the axes of the workmen of King Hezekiah were sharp and clear on the stone.

The first hundred feet were simple, but then the tunnel became low and we had to walk bent double. There was also pot-holes in which we suddenly sank well over the knee. The total length of the tunnel is over a quarter of a mile, , so that I had plenty of time to regret my decision to explore it and admire the common sense of all those people who refused to go with me!

What a weird experience it was, this slow splash through a tunnel which Isaiah must have seen in the making, a tunnel cut seven hundred years before the birth of Christ in the shadow of the hill on which Solomon's temple was still standing…

☆ ☆ ☆

We climbed out into the Kedron Valley. I looked up and saw, high above me to the left, the walls of Jerusalem with the moonlight over them. As we went on through the lonely valley with its crowded tombs at the foot of the Mount of Olives we saw the little walled Garden of Gethsemane, with the light of the moon falling between its cypress trees and lying across its quiet paths.

In the Steps of the Master (Rich & Cowan, London, 1934)

Night and moonlight, 1863
H.D. THOREAU

Many men walk by day; few walk by night. It is a very different season. Take a July night for instance. About ten o'clock – when man is asleep – and day fairly forgotten – the beauty of moonlight is seen over lonely pastures when cattle are silently feeding. On all sides novelties present themselves. Instead of the sun, there are the moon and stars; instead of the wood-thrush, there is the whip-poor-will; instead of butterflies in the meadows, fire-flies, winged sparks of fire! Who would have believed it? What kind of cool deliberate life dwells in those dewy abodes associated with a spark of fire? So man has fire in his eyes, or blood, or brain. Instead of singing birds, the half-throttled note of a cuckoo flying

Methinks that the moment my legs begin to move, my thoughts begin to flow.
H.D. THOREAU

over the creaking of frogs, the intenser dream of crickets. The potato-vines stand upright, the corn grows apace, the bushes loom, the grain-fields are boundless...

The Selected Essays of Henry David Thoreau (Houghton Mifflin, New York, 1906)

The lamplighter, 1939
H.V. MORTON

The lamplighter, with his pole on his shoulder, is already among the ghosts of London. Sometimes, when I look from my window in the evening, I see him emerge from a side street and disappear beneath an old archway.

He is more than ever like a ghost, because there is not a lamp in sight that he could reach with his pole, were it ten times as long. Those lamps are all tall, modern lamps that are lit up by time-clocks or from a main. Still, the lamplighter crosses the street in the evening on some mysterious mission.

I wonder how many people feel, as I do, an affection for lamplighters that dates from the earliest years of childhood. I remember what it felt like to wait, pressing my face against a window-pane, for the moment when he would come with a leisurely stride, leaving little stars and pools of yellow light behind him; and what a lovely moment it was when he would pause opposite to lift the pole and bring the lamp to life.

Rather surprisingly in other parts of London the lamplighter was still at work each evening into the 1950s. I watched him from our flat at the end of the King's Road on a winter's evening as the pole was lifted high and the lights came on ...

Ghosts of London (Methuen, London, 1939)

How the night passed, 1902
HILAIRE BELLOC

As I left the last house of the village I was not secured from loneliness, and when the road began to climb up the hill into the wild and the trees I was wondering how the night would pass.

Doomed for a certain term to walk at night.
WILLIAM SHAKESPEARE, *HAMLET*

With every step upwards a greater mystery surrounded me. A few stars were out, and the brown night mist was creeping along the water below, but there was still light enough to see the road, and even to distinguish the bracken in the deserted hollows. The highway became little better than a lane; at the top of the hill he plunged under tall pines, and was vaulted over with darkness. The kingdoms that have no walls, and are built up of shadows, began to oppress me as the night hardened. Had I had companions, still we would only have spoken in a whisper, and in that dungeon of trees only my own self would not raise its voice within me.

It was full night when I had reached a vague clearing in the woods; right up on the height of that flat hill. This clearing was called "the Fountain of Magdalen". I was so far relieved by the broader sky of the open field that I could wait and rest a little, and there, at last, separate from men, I thought of a thousand things. The air was full of midsummer and its mixture of exaltation and fear cut me off from ordinary living. I now understood why our religion has made sacred this season of the year; why we have, a little later, the night of St John, the fires in the villages, and the old perception of fairies dancing in the rings of the summer grass. A general communion of all things conspires at this crisis of summer against us reasoning men that should live in the daylight and something fantastic possesses those who are foolish enough to watch upon such nights.

The Path to Rome (George Allen, London, 1902)

The desert at night, 1840
W.H. BARTLETT

Travelling through the desert of Sinai to the Convent of Saint Catherine, the artist W.H. Bartlett wandered one evening into the surrounding desert from his camp.

Wander but a few paces from the encampment, and listen in the profound of the solitude to the low and melancholy sigh of the night wind, which sweeps the light surface of the sand, and drifts

I walked barefoot – the only way to walk on a muddy road.
LAURIE GOUGH, *LIGHT ON A MOONLESS NIGHT*

it against the canvas wall of the tent; that breeze, laden with the voice of ages which traverse the old historic desert, and has waved the long grass and stirred the slumbering waters of the ancient fountains when the patriarchs encamped with their flocks. There is a rapture in pacing alone with such fancies among the drifted sand-heaps, and listening to that wild music, till night has fallen upon the wilderness, over which millions of stars, rising up independently from the very edge of the vast horizon, seem quietly brooding.

One may hear, as it were, the solemn pulsation of the universe. No wonder that of old the shepherds of the Desert were star-worshippers.

Jerusalem Revisited, (A. Hall, Virtue & Co, London, 1855)

In the vicinity of Athens, 1858
MARK TWAIN

At eleven o'clock at night, when most of the ship's company were abed, four of us stole softly ashore in a small boat, a clouded moon favouring the enterprise, and started two and two, and far apart, over a low hill, intending to go clear around the Piraeus out of the way of its police. Picking our way so stealthily over that rocky, nettle-grown eminence, made me feel a good deal as if I were on my way somewhere to steal something. My immediate comrade and I talked in an undertone about quarantine laws and their penalties, but we found nothing cheering in the subject.

We made the entire circuit of the town without seeing any body but one man, who stared at us curiously, but said nothing, and a dozen persons slept on the ground before their doors, whom we walked among and never woke – but we woke up dogs enough, in all conscience – we always had one or two barking at our heels, and several times we had as many as ten or twelve at once.

There ain't no surer way to find out whether you like people or hate them than to travel with them. MARK TWAIN

When we had come the whole circuit, and were passing among the houses on the further side of town, the moon came out splendidly, but we no longer feared the light. As we approached a well, near a house, to get a drink, the owner merely glanced at us and went within. He left the quiet, slumbering town at our mercy. I record it here proudly, that we didn't do anything to it.

Seeing no road we took a tall hill to the left of the distant Acropolis for a mark, and steered straight for it over all the obstructions, and over a little rougher piece of country than exists anywhere else outside of the State of Nevada, perhaps. Part of the way was covered with small, loose stones – we trod on six at a time, and they all rolled. Another part of it was dry, loose, newly-ploughed ground. Still another part of it was a long stretch of low grape-vines, which were tanglesome, and which we took to be brambles. The Attic Plain, barring the grape-vines, was a barren, desolate, unpoetical waste – I wonder what it was in Greece's Age of Glory, five hundred years before Christ?

The Innocents Abroad (American Publishing Co, 1869)

On the road to Germany, 1845
BAYARD TAYLOR

Bayard Taylor is one of the very few walkers who acknowledges that, at times, walking can become a somewhat painful activity – he was clearly suffering from blisters on his feet. But, for him, the beauty of the scenery and the fading light compensated for the pain....

The sun had nearly touched the tower on the Kyffhauser when I set out for Artern; but the fields still glowed with heat, and the far blue hills, which I must reach, seemed to grow no nearer, as I plodded painfully along the field roads ...

It is wearisome to tell of a weary journey. The richest fields may be monotonous, and the sweetest pastoral scenery become tame, without change. I looked over the floor of the golden mead, with ardent longing, towards the spire of Artern in the east, and with a faint interest towards the castle of Sachsenberg in the south, perched above a gorge through which the Unstrut breaks

One's destination is never a place, but a new way of seeing things. HENRY MILLER

its way. The sun went down in a splendour of colour, the moon came up like a bronze shield, grain-waggons rolled homewards, men and women flocked into the villages, with rakes and forks on their shoulders, and a cool dusk slowly settled over the great plain, and so I went over the remaining miles, entering the gates of Artern by moonlight.

Views A-foot, or, Europe Seen with a Knapsack and Staff
(Wiley & Putnam, New York, 1846)

By moonlight, 1908
KENNETH GRAHAME

The characters of 'The Wind in the Willows' see the countryside from a different angle than do humans ...

The line of the horizon was clear and hard against the sky, and in one particular quarter it showed black against a silvery climbing phosphorescence that grew and grew. At last, over the rim of the waiting earth the moon lifted with slow majesty, till it swung clear to the horizon and rode off, free of moorings, and once more they began to see surfaces – meadows widespread, and quiet gardens, and the river itself from bank to bank, all softly disclosed, all washed clean of mystery and terror, all radiant again as by day, but with a difference that was tremendous. Their old haunts greeted them again in other raiment, as if they had slipped away and put on this pure new apparel and come quietly back, smiling as they shyly waited to see if they would be recognised again under it.

Fastening their boat to a willow, the friends landed in this silent, silver kingdom, and patiently explored the hedges, the hollow trees, the runnels and their little culverts, the ditches and dry water-ways. Embarking again and crossing over, they worked their way up the stream in this manner, while the moon, serene and detached in a cloudless sky, did what she could, though so far off, to help them in their quest; till her hour came and she sank earthwards reluctantly, and left them, and mystery once more held field and river....

The Wind in the Willows (Methuen, London, 1908)

The only exercise I take is walking behind the coffins of friends who took exercise. PETER O'TOOLE

Through Rotterdam before dawn, 1950
PATRICK LEIGH FERMOR

Setting out on the long journey which would carry him across Europe as the clouds of war were building up, Leigh Fermor landed at the Hook of Holland, and through the snowy night went by train to Rotterdam, arriving at dawn.

I wandered about the silent lanes in exultation. The beetling storeys were nearly joining overhead; then the eaves drew away from each other and frozen canals threaded their way through a succession of hump-backed bridges. Snow was piling up on the shoulders of a statue of Erasmus. Trees and masts were dispersed in clumps and the polygonal tiers of an enormous and elaborate gothic belfry soared above the steep roofs. As I was gazing, it slowly tolled five.

The lanes opened on the Boomjes, a long quay lined with trees and capstans and this in its turn gave on a wide arm of the Maas and an infinity of dim ships. Gulls mewed and wheeled overhead and dipped into the lamplight, scattering their small footprints on the muffled cobblestones and settled in the rigging of the anchored boats in little explosions of snow. The cafés and sea-men's taverns which lay back from the quay were closed except one which showed a promising line of light. A shutter went up and a stout man in clogs opened a glass door, deposited a tabby on the snow and, turning back, began lighting a stove inside. The cat went in again at once; I followed it and the ensuing fried eggs and coffee, ordered by signs, were the best I had ever eaten …

The landlord asked where I was going: I said, "Constantinople". His eyebrows went up and he signalled me to wait: then he set out two small glasses and filled them with trans-parent liquid from a long stone bottle. We clinked them; he emp-tied his at one gulp, and I did the same. With his wishes for god-speed in my ears and an internal bonfire of Bols and a hand smarting from his valedictory shake, I set off. It was the formal start of my journey.

A Time of Gifts: On Foot to Constantinople (John Murray, London, 1977)

The walls of Istanbul, 1897
RICHARD DAVEY

I returned to the walls again and again. I saw them at sunset, when they were as crimson as the blood which so often, in bygone times, reddened the waters of their broad moat – at noonday when the yellow stones of which they are built shimmered in the golden light – and after nightfall, when the weird beauty of the scene was enhanced a hundred-fold by the glory of an Eastern moon. Then all the tall cypresses, black in the shade of night, contrasted vividly with the thousands of fantastic Turkish tombstones, white as ghosts, that stretched for miles back into the country, while the towers, gates, walls and bastions – three rows of them – stood, here in gloomy grandeur, and there, bathed in the radiance of that exquisite light. A thousand nightingales sang in the laurel bushes that cover the base of the prodigious wall which screens the living city from the city of the dead. How beautiful it all was! How full of memories – how calm – how utter in its peace! How overwhelming in its sadness! A gigantic monument to fallen dynasties, faiths and peoples.

All the time, we walked along, on that lovely night in June – meeting no one – with the long stretch of wall on one side, and the great cemetery on the other, certain serene movements in Beethoven's 'Moonlight Sonata' stole into my memory; and whenever, since then, that divine melody falls on my ear, the stately walls and towers of Stambul, and the field of death beyond them, rise vividly before me and haunt me for hours afterwards. And a hundred times a hundred have I recalled, with feelings of delight, not unmingled with sadness, that never-to-beforgotten moonlight saunter by the walls of Constantinople.

The Sultan and his Subjects (Dutton, New York, 1897)

The end is where we start from.
T.S. ELIOT, *FOUR QUARTETS*

APPENDIX A – THE WALKERS

"**Amelia**" is the pseudonym of one contributor to a private women's magazine called Co-operative Correspondence Club (CCC), set up in 1935 and produced fortnightly for nearly 60 years.

Guy Arnold (born 1932), writer and lecturer, followed George Borrow's route through Spain and has walked across Europe to Turkey.

Jane Austen (1775-1817) was an English novelist whose works of romantic fiction, set among the landed gentry, earned her a place as one of the most widely read writers in English literature.

Baedeker, founded by **Karl Baedeker** (1801-1859) in 1827, is a German publisher and pioneer in the business of worldwide travel guides.

Jenna Bailey (fl.1970s) is the biographer of the Co-operative Correspondence Club, a group of Englishwomen who for years circulated a private magazine to which each added news (see "Amelia" and Jenna Bailey's book, *Can Any Mother Help Me?* (Faber & Faber, London, 2007)

W.H. Bartlett (1809-1854), a widely travelled topographical artist, described and illustrated his journeys.

Henry Walter Bates (1825-1892) spent years in the Amazon region, identifying insects, and became an important supporter of Darwin's theories.

Hilaire Belloc (1870-1953), Anglo-French poet and author, wrote about people, places and Catholicism.

Isabella Bird (1831-1904) travelled widely, wrote several accounts of her travels and became the first female member of the Royal Geographical Society.

George Borrow (1803-1881) travelled widely in Britain, Russia and the Near East, and is best known for his *Wild Wales* and *The Bible in Spain* – celebrating the open air and vagrant life.

James Boswell (1740-1795) was a Scottish lawyer, diarist, and author, best known for his biography of Samuel Johnson.

F.G. Brabant (fl. 1906) was a naturalist and writer.

Anne Bridge (1889-1974) was a novelist, biographer and travel writer.

Bill Bryson (born 1951) is an American author of travel books. He lives in Britain and is the current Chancellor of Durham University.

E.L. Butcher (fl. 1910) was the wife of a cleric in Egypt.

Deborah Cadbury is an award-winning author and BBC television producer specialising in fundamental issues of science and history, and their effects on modern society.

Lewis Carroll (Charles Lutwidge Dodgson) (1832-1898) was a writer, mathematician, Anglican deacon and photographer. His most famous writings are *Alice's Adventures in Wonderland* and its sequel *Through the Looking-Glass.*

Evliya Çelebi (1611-1682) was a Turkish traveller who journeyed through the Ottoman Empire.

W.B. Cheadle (1836-1910) was a doctor who, together with William Fitzwilliam (Viscount Milton), travelled in Canada in 1863.

Dame Agatha Christie (1890-1976), detective novelist, and her second husband, archaeologist, Max Mallowen, travelled in the Middle East.

John Clare (1793-1864), was an under-gardener, attended night school, wrote songs, became an impoverished vagrant, yet published his poetry.

Lady Evelyn Cobbold (1867-1963), a Scottish traveller, converted to Islam, and, at the age of 66, performed the pilgrimage to Mecca.

Anthony Collett (1877-1929) wrote *The Changing Face of England*, illuminating the variety of scene and country in Britain.

Charlie Connelly (born 1970) is a successful travel writer, broadcaster and author of *Attention all Shipping: A Journey round the Shipping Forecast.*

Captain James Cook (1728-1779) circumnavigated the world in 1771 and charted the coasts of New Zealand, Australia, the islands of the Pacific and the coast of North America.

Charles James Cornish (1858-1906) was naturalist, school master, and writer on natural history.

Robert Curzon (1810-1873) travelled in the Middle East in search of manuscripts, and worked on Middle Eastern boundary commissions.

Richard Davey (fl. 1890s) travelled in Turkey in 1895 and wrote "one of the most thorough accounts of contemporary Turkey. He brought the country alive for the reader who had never been there."

Annabel Davis-Goff (born 1942) is an Irish writer best known for her memoir *Walled Gardens*.

Daniel Defoe (1661-1731), journalist, novelist and historian, in 1719 published his best known work: *Robinson Crusoe*.

Amelia Edwards (1831-1892), novelist and travel writer, is best known for her work in Egyptology.

Peter Fleming (1907-1971), elder brother of James Bond author, Ian Fleming, was a British adventurer and travel writer, documenting his extensive travels in Brazil and Asia.

Winifred Fortescue (1888-1951) married Sir John Fortescue, the British historian of World War I, and lived in France.

Robert Fortune (1812-1880), botanist, wrote about his travels in India, China and the Himalayas.

Peter Francis (fl. 1920) worked in a Soviet factory after the Russian Revolution.

Jane, Lady Franklin (1791-1875) was an early Tasmanian pioneer, traveller and second wife of the explorer John Franklin.

Johann Wolfgang von Goethe (1749-1832) was a German writer, artist, and politician with a prolific body of work.

Kenneth Grahame (1859-1932) worked at the Bank of England but is remembered for his children's book, *The Wind in the Willows*.

Thomas Gray (1716-1771), poet and professor of history and modern languages at Cambridge.

Thomas Hardy (1840-1928) was a poet, architect and novelist.

Howard Hopley wrote of his travels up the Nile in the 1860s in *Under Egyptian Palms*.

Richard Jefferies (1848-1887), naturalist, novelist and journalist, is best remembered for his children's book, *Bevis*.

Adam Steinmetz Kennard wrote of his time in the Holy Land in the mid 19th century.

A.W. Kinglake (1809-1891) is best known as historian of the Crimean War, but also for his account of his Eastern travels, *Eothen*.

Mary Kingsley (1862-1900), traveller and writer, formed valuable zoological collections in West Africa (1893-5).

Marjorie Kinnan Rawlings (1896-1953) was an American author who wrote novels with rural themes and settings, including *The Yearling*.

Rudyard Kipling (1865-1936), born in India, wrote stories and verse. He is best remembered today for *The Jungle Books* and *Just So Stories*.

Patrick Leigh Fermor (1915-2011) was a soldier, scholar, writer and intrepid traveller.

Pierre Loti (1850-1923), French naval officer, wrote novels about the places he visited and published his autobiography.

Annie C. Macleod (1812-1872) intended her book *Half Hours in the Holy Land* as "an abbreviated reprint" of her father's *Eastward* – about his 1864 journey in the Holy Land.

Harriet Martineau (1802-1876), novelist, writer, economist, who, despite poor health, travelled in Egypt and America.

Viscount Milton (William Wentworth Fitzwilliam) (1839-1877) was a politician and explorer who travelled across Canada.

J.B.S. Morritt (1771-1843) travelled in Greece and Asia Minor in 1794-6, and was a founder of London's Travellers Club.

H.V. Morton (1892-1979) was a prolific travel writer, biographer and journalist.

Eric Newby (1919-2006) was a travel writer and adventurer. For many years he was the travel editor of *The Observer* newspaper.

Florence Nightingale (1820-1910) was a celebrated British social reformer and statistician, and the founder of modern nursing.

George Orwell (Eric Blair) (1903-1950) served in the Spanish Civil War and was a writer of literary criticism, poetry, fiction and polemical journalism.

Oxford Pedestrians Association cares for the concerns of walkers and other pedestrians.

J.H.B. Peel (1913-1983), journalist, author and poet, wrote about the countryside.

J.B. Priestley (1894-1984) writer, playwright, essayist and novelist, wrote *An English Journey* in 1934.

William Cowper Prime (1825–1905) was an American journalist, art historian and travel writer who published *Boat Life in Egypt and Nubia* and *Tent Life in the Holy Land* based on his experiences there.

Eustace A. Reynolds-Ball (fl.1900) was a traveller who wrote of his experiences in Egypt.

Lilias Rider Haggard (1892-1968), daughter of the novelist Henry Rider Haggard, wrote about the English countryside.

Frederic Riley (fl. 1930) wrote about the Yorkshire town of Settle and its surroundings.

John Ruskin (1819-1900), author, artist and social reformer, influenced taste and ideas.

The Ranee Margaret of Sarawak (1849-1936) wrote of her life as queen-consort of the second White Rajah of Sarawak, Charles Anthony Johnson Brooke.

Ernest Shackleton (1874-1922) was a polar explorer who led three British expeditions to the Antarctic.

Raja Shehadeh (born 1951) wrote the prize-winning *Palestinian Walks*. He is a lawyer who once walked freely through his country.

Willem Schellinks (1627-1678) was a Dutch artist who visited France in 1646 and England in 1661 keeping careful and observant diaries of his journeys.

Constance Sitwell (fl. 1920-30) was an English traveller and writer.

Sir George Sitwell (1860–1943), writer and Conservative politician, was a great gardening enthusiast.

Osbert Sitwell (1892-1969), poet, novelist, travel and short story writer, is best remembered for his autobiography, *Left Hand, Right Hand (1944-50)*.

Tobias Smollett (1721-1771), novelist and doctor, wrote *A History of England* (1753).

Christopher Somerville has been writing about his slow-paced exploration of Britain, Ireland and Europe for over thirty years.

Roger W. Squires writes about walking in *English Country Lanes* and *Canal Walks*.

E.S. Stevens wrote vividly of her time in the Sudan.

Robert Louis Stevenson (1850-1894) was a Scottish novelist, poet, and travel writer. A literary celebrity during his lifetime, Stevenson now ranks among the 26 most translated authors in the world.

Bayard Taylor (1825-1878) was an American traveller, poet and literary critic, who spent much of his time close to nature.

Flora Thompson (1876-1947), novelist and poet, is best remembered for her books about '*Lark Rise*', an Oxfordshire village.

James Thomson (1700-1748) was a Scottish poet and playwright, known for his masterpiece *The Seasons* and the lyrics of *Rule, Britannia!*.

William McClure Thomson (fl. mid-1800s) arrived in Beirut as a young missionary in the 1830s and finished writing *The Land and the Book* 25 years later.

Henry David Thoreau (1817-1862) was an American naturalist, poet, philosopher and writer.

Colin Thubron (born 1939) is an award-winning travel writer and novelist. In 2010 he became President of the Royal Society of Literature.

Mark Twain (Samuel Clemens) (1835-1910) was an American journalist best remembered for *The Adventures of Huckleberry Finn*.

Elizabeth von Arnim (1866-1941) was the English wife of a German count who began her literary career writing of life on his estate in Germany.

Alfred Wainwright (1907-1991) was a British fellwalker, guidebook author and illustrator who devised the Coast to Coast Walk, the 192-mile long-distance footpath across northern England.

Alfred Russel Wallace (1823-1913) was a British naturalist, explorer, geographer, anthropologist and biologist.

Ward, Lock & Co was a publishing house that became renowned for its Red Guides from the 1880s onwards.

Arthur E.P. Weigall (1880-1934) was an English Egyptologist, journalist and author whose works span the whole range from histories of Ancient Egypt through historical biographies, guide-books, popular novels, screenplays and lyrics.

Gilbert White (1720-1793), was a pioneering naturalist and curate of Selborne in Hampshire. His still-influential *Natural History of Selborne* was published in 1789.

Dorothy Wordsworth (1771-1855), sister of the poet William Wordsworth, lived with him in the Lake District. Her observations sometimes appeared in his poetry.

William Wordsworth (1770-1850) was a major English Romantic poet whose work was influenced by a love of nature, particularly that of the Lake District. He became Poet Laureate in 1843.

Chiang Yee (1903-1977), a Chinese scholar, came to England in the 1930s and wrote of the country from an original background – '*The Silent Traveller* …'.

APPENDIX B – BIBLIOGRAPHY

Addison, William *Suffolk* (Robert Hale, London, 1950)

Arnold, Guy *In the Footsteps of George Borrow: A journey through Spain and Portugal* (Signal Books, Oxford, 2007)

Austen, Jane *Pride and Prejudice* (T. Egerton, London, 1813)

Baedeker, Karl *Baedeker's Great Britain* (Karl Baedeker, Leipzig, 1890)

Bailey, Jenna *Can Any Mother Help Me?* (Faber & Faber, London, 2007)

Bartlett, W.H. *Jerusalem Revisited* (A. Hall, Virtue & Co, London, 1855)

Bates, Henry Walter *The Naturalist on the River Amazons* (Murray, London, 1863)

Belloc, Hilaire *The Path to Rome* (George Allen, London, 1902)

Bird, Isabella *Letters to Henrietta* (The Leisure Hour, London, 1879)

Blackwood's Magazine *Blackwood's Magazine* (1891)

Borrow, George *Wild Wales: Its People, Language and Scenery* (John Murray, London, 1862) and *The Bible in Spain* (John Murray, London, 1843)

Boswell, James *The Journal of a Tour to the Hebrides* (J. Debrett, London, 1785)

Brabant, F.G. *Oxfordshire* (Methuen, London, 1906)

Branch, C.R. *Cotswold and Vale: or Glimpses of Past and Present in Gloucestershire* (Norman, Sawyer & Co, Cheltenham, 1909)

Bridge, Ann *Peking Picnic* (Little, Brown & Co, Boston, 1932)

Bridges, Philippa *A Walk-about in Australia* (Hodder & Stoughton, London, 1925)

Bryson, Bill *A Walk in the Woods: Rediscovering America on the Appalachian Trail* (HarperCollins, 1998)

Butcher, E.L. *Things Seen in Egypt* (Seeley, London, 1910)

Carroll, Lewis *Alice's Adventures in Wonderland* (Macmillan, London, 1865)

Çelebi, Evliya *An Ottoman Traveller: Selections from the Book of Travels of Evliya Çelebi* (Eland Books, London, 2010)

Christie, Agatha *Third Girl* (The Crime Club Collins, London, 1966)

Clare, John *The Moorhen's Nest* (1820)

Cobbold, Lady Evelyn *Wayfarers in the Libyan Desert* (Arthur Humphreys, London, 1912)

Collet, Anthony *The Changing Face of England* (Nisbet, London, 1926)

Connelly, Charlie *Attention all Shipping: A Journey round the Shipping Forecast* (Little Brown, London, 2004)

Cook, Captain James *The Journals of Captain Cook, 1768-79* (Strahan & Cadell, London, 1773)

Cornish, C.J. *Wild England of Today and the Wildlife in it* (Seeley, London, 1895)

Curzon, Robert *Armenia* (John Murray, London, 1854)

Davey, Richard *The Sultan and his Subjects* (Dutton, New York, 1897)

Davis-Goff, Annabel *Walled Gardens: Scenes from an Anglo-Irish Childhood* (Knopf, New York, 1989)

Defoe, Daniel *Life and Adventures of Robinson Crusoe* (W Taylor, London, 1719)

Dickens, Charles *Oliver Twist* (Richard Bentley, London, 1838)

Edwards, Amelia *Untrodden Peaks and Unfrequented Valleys* (Longman's, Green & Co, London, 1873)

Fleming, Peter *Brazilian Adventure* (Jonathan Cape, London, 1933)

Fortescue, Winifred *Perfume from Provence* (Blackwood, Edinburgh, 1935)

Fortune, Robert *A Journey to the Tea Countries of China and India* (John Murray, London, 1852)

Francis, Peter *I worked in a Soviet Factory* (Jarrolds, London, 1938)

Franklin, Lady Jane *Some Private Correspondence, Tasmania, Vols xvii & xviii* (ed. Geo Mackaness, 1837-45)

Goethe, Johann Wolfgang von *Italian Journey 1786-1788* (Collins, London, 1962)

Grahame, Kenneth *The Wind in the Willows* (Methuen, London, 1908)

Gray, Thomas *Journal of his Tour in the Lake District* (1775)

Hardy, Thomas *Tess of the d'Urbervilles* (Macmillan, London, 1891)

Hopley, Howard *Under Egyptian Palms* (1869)

Kennard, Adam Steinmetz *Eastern Experiences* (Longmans, London, 1855)

Kinglake, A.W. *Eothen; or Traces of travel brought home from the East* (John Ollivier, London, 1844)

Kingsley, Mary *Travels in West Africa* (Macmillan & Co, London, 1897)

Kipling, Rudyard *From Sea to Sea; Letters of Travel, Volume 2*, (1920) *The Day's Work* (Macmillan & Co, London, 1898)

Leigh Fermor, Patrick *A Time of Gifts: On Foot to Constantinople* (John Murray, London, 1977)

Loti, Pierre *Istanbul* (Casterman, Paris, 1992)

MacLeod, Annie C. *Half Hours in the Holy Land* (The Half Hour Library, London, 1884)

Margaret of Sarawak, The Ranee *My Life in Sarawak* (Methuen, London, 1913)

Martineau, Harriet *Eastern Life* (Edward Moxon, London, 1848)

Milton, Viscount and Dr Cheadle *The North-West Passage by Land* (Cassell, London, 1865)

Morritt J.B.S. *The Letters of John B.S. Morritt of Rokeby* (Cambridge UP, 1914)

Morton, H.V. *Ghosts of London* (Methuen, London, 1939), *H.V. Morton's London* (Methuen, London, 1940), *In the Steps of the Master* (Rich & Cowan, London, 1934)

Newby, Eric *A Short Walk in the Hindu Kush* (Secker & Warburg, London, 1958)

Nightingale, Florence *On Mysticism and Eastern Religions, Volume 4* (1851)

Orwell, George *Homage to Catalonia* (Secker and Warburg, London, 1938)

Oxford Pedestrians Association *Oxford on Foot*, (2008)

Peel, J.H.B. *Along the Roman Roads of Britain* (Cassell, London, 1971)

Priestley, J.B. *Rain Upon Godshill, A Further Chapter of Autobiography* (Heinemann, London, 1939), *English Journey* (W Heinemann in association with V. Gollancz, London, 1934)

Prime, William C. *Boat Life in Egypt and Nubia* (Harper & Bros, New York, 1857)

Rawlings, Marjorie Kinnan *The Yearling* (Charles Scribner's Sons, New York, 1938)

Reynolds-Ball, Eustace A. *The City of the Caliphs* (Estes & Laurait, Boston, 1897)

Rider Haggard, Lilias *A Country Scrap-Book* (Faber & Faber, London, 1950), *Norfolk Notebook* (Faber & Faber, London, 1946)

Riley, Frederic *The Settle District and North West Yorkshire Dales A Practical Guide Book for the Visitor and Tourist* (Settle, 1923)

Ruskin, John *The Seven Lamps of Architecture: The Lamp of Memory* (Smith, Elder & Co, London, 1849)

Schellinks, William *The Journal of William Schellinks' Travels in England, 1661-1663* (Royal Historical Society, London, 1993)

Shackleton, Ernest *South: The story of Shackleton's last expedition, 1914-1917* (Heinemann, London, 1919)

Shehadeh, Raja *Palestinian Walks: Forays into a Vanishing Landscape* (Profile Books, London, 2007)

Sitwell, Constance *Petals and Places* (Jonathan Cape, London, 1935)

Sitwell, Sir George *On the Making of Gardens* (John Murray, London, 1909)

Sitwell, Osbert *Laughter in the Next Room: Left Hand, Right Hand Vol IV,* (Macmillan, London, 1949), *The Scarlet Tree: Being the Second Volume of 'Left Hand, Right Hand!'* (Macmillan, London, 1946)

Smollett, Tobias *Travels through France and Italy* (R. Baldwin, London, 1766)

Somerville, Christopher *Twelve Literary Walks* (WH Allen, London, 1985)

Squires, Roger W. & **Lovett Jones, G.** *Canal Walks* (Hutchinson, London, 1985)

Stevens, E.S. *My Sudan Year* (Mills & Boon, London, 1912)

Stevenson, Robert Louis *Travels with a Donkey in the Cévennes* (Kegan Paul & Co, London, 1879), *Virginibus Puerisque, and Other Papers* (C Kegan Paul, London, 1881)

Taylor, Bayard *At Home and Abroad: A Sketchbook of Life, Scenery and Men* (George P Putnam, New York, 1860), *Eldorado, or, Adventures in the Path of Empire* (George P Putnam, New York, 1850), *Views A-foot, or, Europe Seen with a Knapsack and Staff* (Wiley & Putnam, New York, 1846)

The Table Book (William Hone, London, 1827)

Thompson, Flora *Still Glides the Stream* (Oxford University Press, 1948)

Thomson, James *The Seasons* (P.W. Tomkins, London, 1797)

Thomson, Rev W.M. *The Land and the Book* (Harper & Bros, New York, 1859)

Thoreau, H.D. *The Selected Essays of Henry David Thoreau* (Houghton Mifflin, New York, 1906)

Thubron, Colin *To a Mountain in Tibet* (Chatto & Windus, London, 2011)

Twain, Mark *A Tramp Abroad* (American Publishing Co, 1880), *The Innocents Abroad* (American Publishing Co, 1869)

von Arnim, Elizabeth *The Solitary Summer* (Macmillan & Co, London, 1899)

Wainwright, Alfred *Fellwalking with Wainwright: 18 of the author's favourite walks in Lakeland* (Michael Joseph, London, 1984)

Wallace, Alfred Russel *The Malay Archipelago: The Land of the Orang-utan, and the Bird of Paradise* (Harper & Bros, New York, 1869)

Ward, Lock & Company, Ltd. *Ward Lock Red Guide: The Yorkshire Dales* (Ward, Lock & Co, London, 1965)

Weigall, Arthur E.P. *Travels in the Upper Egyptian Desert* (Thornton Butterworth, London, 1909)

White, Gilbert *The Natural History of Selborne* (T. Bensley for B. White and Son, London, 1789)

Wordsworth, Dorothy *Journals of Dorothy Wordsworth* (Macmillan, London, 1897)

Wordsworth, William *Poems in Two Volumes: Moods of my Mind* (1807)

Yee, Chiang *The Silent Traveller in London* (Country Life, London, 1938; rpt Signal Books, 2001), *The Silent Traveller in Oxford* (Methuen, London 1944; rpt Signal Books, Oxford 2001)

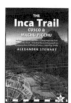

TRAILBLAZER TITLE LIST

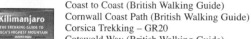

Adventure Cycle-Touring Handbook
Adventure Motorcycling Handbook
Australia by Rail
Australia's Great Ocean Road
Azerbaijan
Coast to Coast (British Walking Guide)
Cornwall Coast Path (British Walking Guide)
Corsica Trekking – GR20
Cotswold Way (British Walking Guide)
Dolomites Trekking – AV1 & AV2
Dorset & Sth Devon Coast Path (British Walking Gde)
Exmoor & Nth Devon Coast Path (British Walking Gde)
Hadrian's Wall Path (British Walking Guide)
Himalaya by Bike – a route and planning guide
Inca Trail, Cusco & Machu Picchu
Japan by Rail
Kilimanjaro – the trekking guide (includes Mt Meru)
Mediterranean Handbook
Morocco Overland (4WD/motorcycle/mountainbike)
Moroccan Atlas – The Trekking Guide
Nepal Trekking & The Great Himalaya Trail
New Zealand – The Great Walks
North Downs Way (British Walking Guide)
Norway's Arctic Highway
Offa's Dyke Path (British Walking Guide)
Overlanders' Handbook – worldwide driving guide
Peddars Way & Norfolk Coast Path (British Walking Gde)
Pembrokeshire Coast Path (British Walking Guide)
Pennine Way (British Walking Guide)
The Ridgeway (British Walking Guide)
Siberian BAM Guide – rail, rivers & road
The Silk Roads – a route and planning guide
Sahara Overland – a route and planning guide
Scottish Highlands – The Hillwalking Guide
Sinai – the trekking guide
South Downs Way (British Walking Guide)
Tour du Mont Blanc
Trans-Canada Rail Guide
Trans-Siberian Handbook
Trekking in the Everest Region
Trekking in Ladakh
The Walker's Anthology
The Walker's Haute Route – Mont Blanc to Matterhorn
West Highland Way (British Walking Guide)

For more information about Trailblazer and our
expanding range of guides, for guidebook updates or
for credit card mail order sales visit our website:

www.trailblazer-guides.com

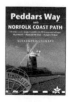

INDEX